AN ADMINISTRATOR'S HANDBOOK
OF SPECIAL EDUCATION
A Guide to Better Education for the Handicapped

An Administrator's Handbook of Special Education

A GUIDE TO BETTER EDUCATION FOR THE HANDICAPPED

By

MORVIN A. WIRTZ, Ed.D.
Professor of Special Education
College of Education
Western Michigan University
Kalamazoo, Michigan

CHARLES C THOMAS · PUBLISHER
Springfield · Illinois · U.S.A.

Published and Distributed Throughout the World by
CHARLES C THOMAS • PUBLISHER
Bannerstone House
301-327 East Lawrence Avenue, Springfield, Illinois, U.S.A.

© 1977, by CHARLES C THOMAS • PUBLISHER
ISBN 0-398-03542-3
Library of Congress Catalog Card Number: 75-44128

With THOMAS BOOKS *careful attention is given to all details of
manufacturing and design. It is the Publisher's desire to present books
that are satisfactory as to their physical qualities and artistic possibilities
and appropriate for their particular use.* THOMAS BOOKS *will be
true to those laws of quality that assure a good name and good will.*

Printed in the United States of America
W-2

Library of Congress Cataloging in Publication Data
Wirtz, Morvin A
    An administrator's handbook of special education.

    Bibliography: p.
    Includes index.
    1. Handicapped children—Education—United States.
I. Title. [DNLM: 1. Education, Special. 2. Organization
and administration. 3. Handicapped. LC4015 V799a]
LC4031.W57   371.9'0973   75-44128
ISBN 0-398-03542-3

DEDICATION

N o ONE WRITES A volume such as this handbook without the direct and indirect influence of countless numbers of other people and I am no exception. Therefore, I dedicate this book to the thousands of handicapped children and their parents with whom I have worked over the years and to those leaders in special education (including those studying to be leaders) who have been my sounding board for ideas and professional practices. However, my greatest debt is to my wife, June, for without her persistent encouragement this volume might never have been completed.

MAW

PREFACE

ADMINISTRATORS OF THE public schools of America generally receive little or no formal instruction in the art of programming for the handicapped children and youth to be found in their schools. It is only recently that one finds an occasional reference to the handicapped in books which are aimed at the general administrator. Is it any wonder then that the parents of handicapped children and youth have had to develop a degree of militancy to get the attention of their communities so that their children receive even a modicum of service?

The "club" used by parents is the due process protection given to them and their children by the courts. As with the proverbial mule whose attention was obtained by the use of a two-by-four, society is now paying attention; the problem now is to give the "critter" an order to begin to move toward some specific place. How can such an order be given in the field of special education if those responsible for giving the order are not sure if they should go forward, backward, to the right, or to the left?

My experience has been that most administrators (and boards of education, for that matter) are sincerely interested in doing what is right for handicapped children and youth, but they are somewhat confused when confronted with the many program options that are available. I would hope that this book, which is a distillation of almost thirty years of experience (most of it in administrative positions dealing with handicapped children and youth) will be of help to those of you who are searching for a direction in which to go. I also hope it will be an aid to those of you have found a direction, but who have found the road strewn with obstacles and misleading turns.

I have attempted to address myself to the most frequently asked questions and to those problems which pop up most frequently in the administration of programs for the handicapped. I have lived through the implementation of almost every suggestion made in this book and can give my personal testimony as to their effectiveness.

For those of you who are training to be administrators of special education or are already active in the field and are using this book as a resource, I can only hope that you will find it useful in expanding your professional sights. I also hope that you will have as much excitement in your professional life as I have had in mine. May that excitement never die!

CONTENTS

AN ADMINISTRATOR'S HANDBOOK OF SPECIAL EDUCATION

A Guide to Better Education for the Handicapped

CHAPTER ONE_ _ _ _ _ _ _ _ _

INTRODUCTION

— — — — — — — — — — — — — —

Special education has been a fact of life in some of the public schools of this country since the late 1800's. In spite of such a long history of service to handicapped children and youth, the federal government reported that in Fiscal Year 1968 over half the children who needed service were not receiving it. The national figures show that there were 5,961,000 handicapped children of school age needing service; 2,139,000 were receiving the service and 3,822,000 were not.[1] The author can only account for such a deplorable condition by surmising that many of those responsible for mounting programs were not aware of what *could* be done, or did not have the will to carry out the development of programs. Traditionally, the training of school administrators does not include specific training in administering programs for the handicapped in spite of the fact that the majority of states have mandatory special education laws. Is it any wonder then, that many programs are never started or are administered by persons with no real expertise in such matters?

There have been thousands of technical articles and books written on the subject of the education of the handicapped, but little has been written to guide school boards, superintendents, curriculum consultants, and others who may be responsible for setting policy, through the intricacies of such a venture. There have been a few monographs written, which will be referred to later, but a close perusal of these will soon indicate that most have been written by persons who have had little real experience in actually operating a major program for the handicapped.

The time seems ripe to examine practices which, in many

3

instances, have grown like Topsy and which have not been evaluated to any great extent. Professional special educators have been expanding programs, usually by bifurcation and usually for reasons which seem perfectly valid at the moment, but which in reality have become a professional trap from which there seems to be no escape except to start still more types of programs. The result has been the development of an amazing complex of services known as Special Education in which one finds special classes, resource rooms, integrated programs, itinerant programs, special consultants of various types, orientation and mobility specialists, social workers, psychologists, child development specialists, supervisors, and directors. Each of these categories of professionals has its own training program, certification and, in many states, a complicated reimbursement formula. All of this is done for children who have been divided into such categories as slow learners, educable mentally retarded, moderately retarded, trainable mentally retarded, custodial mentally retarded,* crippled or orthopedically handicapped, blind, partially sighted, deaf, hard of hearing, aphasic, brain-injured, neurologically handicapped, perceptually handicapped, emotionally disturbed, learning disabled, speech handicapped, and combinations of these lumped together as multiply handicapped. Each of these areas has its coterie of professional specialists who fit into the program picture mentioned but frequently require a special training program. Is it little wonder, then, that school districts which are new to the business of providing programs for the handicapped frequently find the welter of options so overwhelming that the general educators in charge have difficulty in knowing where to start?

On the other hand, there are those general educators who claim that they do not need special education because they believe that they are taking care of all of the handicapped children within their jurisdiction in the regular classes. One can only wonder how they have managed to convince the parents of children such as the severely cerebral palsied that they should

---

* In some states, the term *handicapped* is used. A still further development is the use of the term *impaired* instead of handicapped.

do *something* with their children other than send them to the schools, because these children obviously cannot be cared for, much less educated, in regular classes. It has been the author's experience that, in most instances, these more severely handicapped children, whatever their handicap, have been systematically excluded from school. This *system* will work where the parents have adequate financial resources to place their children in private facilities, or where the parents are so unsophisticated that they do not know what should be available. Those days are about over, however. With the improvement in communication, the formation of associations of parents, and the decisions of the courts, schools, no matter what their size or makeup, are being pressured to provide services to all children, even those thought to be unsuitable for school attendance even a few years ago. In class action suits, the courts are forcing reluctant school boards and administrators to provide services. A school which reacts to pressure to provide new programs will usually find that it is providing a program which is not in keeping with any organized plan and which may not be in keeping with the long-range goals which characterize well-run systems.

In this book, the author will provide information about the currently accepted options which are available to most professionals in the field. Some innovations will be suggested which will make it possible for the general school administrator, as well as special education directors, to act in a creative manner in the development and improvement of programs for handicapped children.

PHILOSOPHY

Most professional educators, when asked whether they have a philosophy of education, readily admit that they do, and when pressed still further, many would be willing to write a paragraph or two on the subject. These paragraphs usually fall into the pattern of indicating that all children have a right to an education and that each should be viewed as an individual with individual needs and that the schools have a responsibility to meet these needs. Occasionally someone will refer to John Dewey or the

1930 White House Conference on Children and Youth, but as a whole, the responses clearly show that the professionals are talking about a major objective of the schools in working with children and that they are not really talking about a philosophy of education.

In similar fashion, when special educators are asked to express their philosophy of special education, they fall back on the same platitude: "All children have the right to an education within the limits of their capacity to learn." At this point they usually begin discussing techniques for educating children to the limits of their abilities rather than examining the education of handicapped children as part of the total educational milieu. This fact is evident in the series of articles that appeared in the journal, *Exceptional Children*, several years ago.[2-10]

Dewey does have something to say to special educators even though he was not addressing himself to them in his writings. He said:

> The widening of the area of shared concerns and the liberation of a greater diversity of personal capacities which characterize a democracy are not, of course, the product of deliberation and conscious effort. On the contrary, they were caused by the development of modes of manufacture and commerce, travel, migration, and inter-communication which flowed from the command of science over natural energy. But after greater individualization on one hand, and a broader community of interest on the other, have come into existence, it is a matter of deliberate effort to sustain and extend them. Obviously, a society to which stratification into separate classes would be fatal, must see to it that intellectual opportunities are accessible to all on equable and easy terms. A society marked off into classes need be specially attentive only to the education of its ruling elements. A society which is mobile, which is full of channels for the distribution of a change occurring anywhere, must see to it that its members are educated to personal initiative and adaptability. Otherwise, they will be overwhelmed by the changes in which they are caught and whose significance or connections they do not perceive. The result will be a confusion in which a few will appropriate to themselves the results of the blind and externally directed activities of others.[11]

The fact is that good educational philosophy is good for *all* children, whether they are the "kids across the street" or a class of handicapped children. The same can be said of the commonly accepted objectives of helping children attain economic self-sufficiency, self-realization, human interaction, and civic responsibility. Obviously, this applies to all children, handicapped and nonhandicapped alike.

The author summarizes the overall educational aspiration for children, handicapped and nonhandicapped, as a process that prepares them to lead the "good life." The good life will be different for each individual and will be affected by the social-cultural milieu in which each child lives, the economic circumstances of his home community, the nature and degree of his handicap, and the success or failure of education to prepare him to utilize his potentialities to the utmost. Each part of any daily educational activity has to be viewed from the standpoint of whether or not it contributes to the child's good life. The following diagram shows the progression of each decision of what is done for (or to) a child as the *bits* lead to the good life. A bit which contributes to more than one major objective is perhaps more important than a bit which contributes to only one such objective.

The amount of time available for the professionals to work with a child is limited, and in addition, the capabilities of a given child are limited. Therefore, one must be jealous of the time available and make carefully considered decisions about what specific daily activities one will ask the child to expend his precious time in mastering and eliminate those which are only minimally useful. This does not imply that the professionals should sit in judgment over what a child will become, or what will constitute the good life for any child. However, if professional judgment based on good evidence means anything, certainly tentative judgments can be safely made. If children respond to challenge, there is no reason why new judgments cannot be made and the sights raised proportionately.

Too often the good life for handicapped individuals is seen by the general public, parents, and educators, as paralleling that of a nonhandicapped population. Thus, great effort is made to help the handicapped to function as a normal individual. Certainly, in some aspects of the handicapped person's life this

THE GOOD LIFE

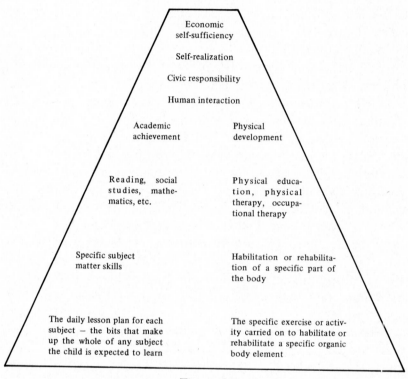

Figure 1.

is possible, while in others it is completely unrealistic. All too often, the aspiration level of a handicapped person is raised by outside pressure to a point where severe emotional disturbances result when it becomes obvious to the individual that he cannot possibly achieve *his* aspiration. More time must be spent in helping the handicapped person see himself as *disabled* (a term preferable to handicapped) and to help him to be the best disabled person possible, but more important, to be comfortable with his view of himself. This means that the curriculum must include, either directly or more subtly, some idea of how a nonhandicapped population views him and how he should react to the nonhandicapped population, whether he is being actively rejected, merely tolerated, or accepted for whatever skills he has. This is not usually viewed as a normal part of the school curriculum, but rather, if it is thought about at all, it is viewed as belonging to some sort of psychotherapy treatment administered by someone outside of the classroom. This misconception must be corrected if handicapped children are to be adequately served in the schools of the United States.

Earlier reference was made to the impact of the social, cultural, and economic milieu on handicapped children. For example, early reports from *Headstart* programs indicated that up to 40 percent of the children enrolled could be considered as having some condition that would mitigate against their having a successful school experience. These conditions ranged from visual problems, hearing defects, nutrition deficiencies, to assorted untreated medical problems. The impact of this information on the field of special education has never been adequately explored. The results of poor nutrition on learning ability is an example of the relationship of widely divergent fields having an impact on the learning process. A child without breakfast may have his blood sugar level so reduced by midmorning that he will not be able to attend to the task at hand no matter what extrinsic motivation is used by the classroom teacher. Thus, these children are frequently referred to, and all too often placed in, classes for the mentally retarded.[12]

It is significant that approximately 20 percent of Title 1 money available under the Elementary and Secondary Education Act (P.L. 89-10) was spent in the first year on providing hot breakfast programs and health-related services. The future of untold thousands of children who are currently being educated as handicapped children rests on efforts such as this to prevent them from being viewed as handicapped with the usual result of lowering the aspiration level of these children. This does not mean to imply that even the best of preventative efforts will eliminate the need for special education. On the contrary, such efforts will free special educators to work with those children who will continue to need special consideration for them to achieve the "good life."

Education in this country will be what the majority of citizens want it to be. If the field of special education is not to be ruled by pressure groups dictating what programs a community will have, or to be directed by the inept, then all school administrators must develop programs that are based on a sound philosophic foundation and with a carefully organized plan of action which shows that educational leadership is being exercised for the best interests of all children, handicapped and non-handicapped.[13]

REFERENCES

1. Second Annual Report: *National Advisory Committee on Handicapped Children, Better Education for Handicapped Children.* U.S. Dept. of H.E.W., U.S. Office of Education, June 30, 1969, p. 14.
2. Mase, Darrell J.: What is special about special education. *Except Child, 19*:3, 95-96, Dec. 1952.
3. Lowenfeld, Berthold: What is special about special education—The child who is blind. *Except Child, 19*:3, 96-102, Dec. 1952.
4. Kirk, Samuel A.: What is special about special education—The child who is mentally handicapped. *Except Child, 19*:4, 138-142, Jan. 1953.
5. Wooden, Harley: What is special about special education—The child who is deaf. *Except Child, 19*:5, 179-182, Feb. 1953.
6. Streng, Alice: What is special about special education—The child who is hard of hearing. *Except Child, 19*:6, 223-226, 244, March 1953.
7. Witty, Paul: What is special about special education—The gifted child. *Except Child, 19*:7, 255-259, April 1953.
8. Mackie, Romaine: What is special about special education—The crippled child. *Except Child, 19*:8, 309-312, May 1953.
9. Bertram, Fredericka M.: What is special about special education—The partially seeing child. *Except Child, 20*:1, 11-15, 27, Oct. 1953.
10. Westlake, Harold: What is special about special education—The speech defective child. *Except Child, 20*:2, 56-60, Nov. 1953.
11. Dewey, John: *Democracy and Education,* 23rd ed. New York, Macmillan, 1950, pp. 101-102.
12. Wirtz, Morvin A.: Expanding concepts in mental retardation and cultural deprivation. *National Journal of Catholic Education, 66*:1, 94-97, Nov. 1969.
13. Wirtz, Morvin and Seay, Maurice: "Special education in community education," in *Community Education: A Developing Concept.* Maurice Seay (Ed.), Midland, Michigan, Pendell Publishing Co., 1974, pp. 313-328.

CHAPTER TWO_ _ _ _ _ _ _ _ _

LEGISLATION

— — — — — — — — — — — — —

THE ROLE OF THE legislative foundation of programs for the education of handicapped children is little understood. Too frequently the prevailing philosophy in a given state is not a reflection of the best professional judgement of forward-thinking individuals; rather, it is circumscribed by the narrowly conceived legislation under which these individuals are forced to create programs. In this chapter the issues of mandatory versus permissive legislation, federal legislation, general versus specific laws, legislative discrimination or exclusion and legislative trends will be discussed. In addition, the creation of legislation, including the roles of pressure groups, will be explored along with what appear to be trends in legislation at the federal and state levels.

Mandatory Versus Permissive Legislation

In recent years the trend in the United States has been away from permissive and toward mandatory legislation. This can be accounted for by the intense desire of organized groups, primarily made up of parents, to insure that each school district provides what these organized groups believe to be necessary educational provisions. One must, however, examine the benefits to be derived from each philosophic position. Mandatory means MUST, so in each mandatory law there will appear at some point the statement that the state, hence the local school districts, must provide some sort of service. Permissive, on the other hand, means MAY and thus, in each piece of permissive legislation, there will appear a statement that the state or local school districts may provide certain services as they choose. On the surface, it would appear that anyone seriously interested in

11

providing complete services would automatically choose mandatory legislation as a philosophic position. There are, however,
some variables to be considered before taking such a position.

For example, in 1947 Missouri passed a mandatory law which
stated that each school district having seven or more handicapped
children must provide special education services. After eleven
years, the school districts of St. Louis County, one of the major
metropolitan areas of the state, were still serving less than 20
percent of the handicapped children in the county. In only a
few instances was this due to any real lack of enthusiasm on
the part of the superintendents in the districts. Instead, the
lack was focused on insufficient money to comply with the law
and a lack of qualified teachers to man the special classrooms.

It would appear that mandatory legislation for special education poses some problems which must be faced along with the
enabling law. These must include adequate financial support
to the districts under the reimbursement formula then in use.
It should also include the training of enough teachers to man
the classrooms along with the inducements necessary to keep
them in the vicinity. Not the least of the problems is the need
for the sometimes specialized facilities necessary for the implementation of special education programs. Still another factor
is the existence of adequate diagnostic personnel to insure children
being properly placed, to say nothing of leadership persons who
have been trained in the techniques of initiating and improving
programs. If a state is ready to make provisions for these
factors, in cooperation with the local school districts, then mandatory legislation is feasible. There is, however, another factor
which is less tangible than personnel and buildings. This is
the *attitude* of school administrators toward being forced to
comply with something with which they or their communities
are not in sympathy. It is difficult to imagine how handicapped
children can be expected to get a "fair shake" in an atmosphere
which is obviously unfavorable and rejecting. These districts
will hire the unfit teachers, consign children to substandard
quarters, and refuse to provide the necessary ancillary services
which handicapped children need. They may well be meeting

the letter of the mandatory law while refusing to accept the spirit which is the essence of working with handicapped children.

Permissive legislation also has its drawbacks. Any school district which has either little desire or minimal financial resources can refuse to initiate or continue special education programs, and unless someone or some group can bring about a change in the school board, those who are in control can continue to make decisions which are adverse to the best interest of handicapped children. Too frequently school districts will start programs and then when money gets tight or a teacher is not readily available, will eliminate a program, usually the most expensive, on a per capita basis. Such actions hardly develop a feeling of security on the part of parents of handicapped children or feelings of worth on the part of the children themselves. The one real advantage of staying with permissive legislation is that when good programs are in operation they tend to continue because of the positive attitude of the school board members and the general school administration. Many excellent programs of special education have been started and continued for fifty years or more under the permissive umbrella, with many of these programs being started long before there was any such thing as legislation dealing specifically with handicapped children. These districts considered that all children under their jurisdiction were worthy of some effort on the part of their home community. One cannot argue with this as a principle. The problems have come with an increasing sophistication of parents about what can be done for their handicapped children and their desire for schools to *do something* and reluctance of schools to provide adequate services. State constitutions do not say that there shall be free public school for all children *except handicapped* children, rather the wording is phrased to mean that there shall be free public education for *all children*. For example, in 1921 parents of several trainable children in Illinois literally forced the schools of their communities, through due legal process, to accept their children in regular classes for nonhandicapped. The school districts had excluded the children from their programs for educable mentally handicapped children, but they found that they could not exclude the children from school altogether. For some reason, these cases were not well known in Illinois. If they had been known, many more trainable children would have been placed in regular classes long before the formation of formal programs for them.

Federal Legislation

The years since 1964 have seen a dramatic increase in the involvement of the federal government in programs of direct import to school age handicapped children. Not all of the legislation for the benefit of the handicapped was written specifically for them; however, it was the intent of Congress that the handicapped participate in the programs fully. In fact, where it became apparent after several years of operation that school districts were not including the handicapped under the authority they had, Congress mandated *set-aside* funds in a number of programs. These programs will be discussed further in this chapter.

The major federal laws which affect school programs for the handicapped are listed below. As these laws are of limited duration, modifications should be monitored carefully as the life of the authority is extended and modified.[1]

ELEMENTARY AND SECONDARY EDUCATION ACT
(P.L. 89-10)

TITLE I: This title provides for financial assistance to local educational agencies for the purpose of running special educational programs in areas having high concentrations of children of low-income families. Most school administrators are familiar with the provisions of this Title; however, little was (or has been) done to make provision for the handicapped even though the original guidelines outlined the possibilities of such programs. The reluctance of school districts to start programs for the handicapped under this authority led to the creation of Title VI of the act in 1966.

TITLE II: Provides for school library resources, textbooks,

and other instructional materials. This Title requires a state plan and the only way the handicapped can participate is if those who develop the plan systematically include some provision for the handicapped. There is little evidence that this has happened.

TITLE III: The original version of this title called for the creation of supplementary educational centers and services where exemplary programs could be tried without regard to existing state restrictions. Some of the most creative programs operated under the authority of this title were developed to aid the handicapped. This Title was subsequently changed so that it too required a state plan and the state education authority had the final say about who received money and approval of programs. The original concept of school districts having some *mad money* and the creativity that it brings has largely been lost because the districts wishing to participate must comply with an overall state plan which may only peripherally address itself to the immediate needs of a given school district. When the law was changed, it was feared that some of the advantage which programs for the handicapped had under the original authority would be lost, so provision was made to set aside 15 percent of the money to be spent on these programs.

TITLE IV: Consolidates the general Office of Education authority for educational research and training with the exception of research and training dealing with the handicapped. Authority for the latter continued to rest under the provisions of P.L. 88-164 as amended by P.L. 89-105. This Title is mentioned here only because the programs operated under this authority may prove to have an impact on handicapped children although not directed at them.

TITLE V: Provides money to strengthen state departments of education by making it possible to employ additional personnel who can provide technical assistance to special education programs throughout a state. One of the major outcomes of this authority has been the development of state-wide master plans for the development of multidistrict, county, or regional special education programs.

Before the guidelines were even written for the original Elementary and Secondary Education Act, an amendment was made to the act (P.L. 89-313) which set aside a percentage of each state's allocation for use in educational facilities operated by agencies of the state such as departments of mental health and mental retardation. This "shot in the arm" made significant changes in the educational programs in many of the states' institutional programs. The process also forced a degree of cooperation between state agencies which had not been evident before.

TITLE VI: This addition to the Elementary and Secondary Act consolidated various programs which had been in existence under previous legislative authorities. In addition, it authorized the provision of federal funds to the states and territories for the express purpose of improving school programs for the handicapped. Amendments have been made in this authority and continue to be made. It behooves every school administrator to keep abreast of such changes. An excellent source of information is a section of the journal, *Exceptional Children*, entitled, "Law Review." The Council for Exceptional Children which publishes *Exceptional Children* also publishes a newsletter entitled *Insight*. This publication is also an excellent source of information about legislation dealing with the handicapped.

General Versus Specific Legislation

An examination of a sampling of state laws which make school provisions for the handicapped (see Appendix) reveals that some of the laws are written in a very general way, almost to the point of saying that schools may (or must) provide school programs for handicapped children under rules and regulations promulgated by the State Superintendent of Education and approved by the State Board of Education. Other state laws are extremely specific. For example, the first law in Wisconsin making it possible for schools to provide programs for the trainable specified that the children must have IQ's between 35 and 49.

The interests of children would seem to be best served by moving away from specific legislation, recognizing the multiplicity of handicaps which children have and imprecision of diagnostic practices. The standard error of the IQ scores cited above, assuming that the original 35 or 49 was correct, actually means that the children so designated will have IQ's which *may* range from about 20 to 60. How, then, can anyone justify admitting one child with a 35 IQ and excluding one with 34, and this is precisely what the law indicates must be done. Countless thousands of diagnosticians have hedged on scores, or should we say, have given a child the "benefit of a doubt," so that a child might be given a chance to succeed in a school setting. Is it not a far better practice to rely on the professional judgment of those who are trained to evaluate the potential of children for success in a wide variety of school settings? In other words, the more specific the law, the less one is apt to find accurate professional judgments. Some of this specificity may have been necessary fifty, twenty-five, or even ten years ago when the need for complete clinical evaluation of children was not as well recognized as it generally is today. In addition, the professionals capable of making these judgments were either nonexistent in many parts of the country or not available to school districts except those in the most sophisticated urban settings.

There is a further reason for putting emphasis on general laws and then spelling out the details in the rules and regulations: A *law* is extremely difficult to get changed once it has been passed. Not because of any unwillingness on the part of lawmakers, but because of the sheer mechanical processes involved in legislative change. On the other hand, rules and regulations can be changed by administrative action of a state superintendent of education and that official's governing body.

Legislative Provision for Expulsion

States generally have a provision somewhere in their school codes which allow school districts to exclude children under special circumstances. All too often, this law has been the vehicle by which handicapped children were systematically excluded from school. This appears to be especially true for children who should be called emotionally disturbed, brain-injured, and the higher level mentally handicapped (especially those for whom the school program was meaningless and for whom no special provisions were made with the result that the children become typical school problems).

Summary Statement

The author cannot emphasize too strongly the need for all school administrators to be aware and keep abreast of federal and state legislation which applies to the handicapped.* This includes those laws directly concerned with the handicapped as well as those which are only of peripheral interest. Creative programming for the handicapped involves a blending of legislative authorities so that the impact of each mandate is brought to bear in setting up comprehensive school programs for them.

REFERENCES

1. Martin, Edwin: Breakthrough for the handicapped: Legislative History. *Except Child, 34*:7, 493-503, March 1968.

---

* See Appendix for a summary of state laws authorizing programs for the handicapped.

CHAPTER THREE_ _ _ _ _ _ _ _

FINANCING SPECIAL EDUCATION

— — — — — — — — — — — — — —

OBSERVING SCHOOL PERSONNEL discuss the financing of special education is akin to watching a group of children playing "hot potato." No one wants to get caught with the hot potato of special education for fear that he will have to pay the price of operating programs. One must raise the question of who *should* pay the cost of educating handicapped children. Much of the procrastination associated with starting new programs (or continuing old ones for that matter) stems from the reluctance or perceived inability of boards of education to put any local tax money into such programs. The feeling of many local administrators and boards of education is that special education is the responsibility of the state or federal government—*anyone* except the local district. This attitude is hard to defend if one takes an unbiased look at the problem. Are children any less the responsibility of the local district merely because they are handicapped? Their parents reside in a local district and pay their school taxes in that district. If programs were uniformly provided there would be a relatively uniform distribution of such programs throughout the local districts of a given state. The real problem is not the *responsibility* as such, but the dearth of tax money to operate any school program.

One can only conclude that the actual responsibility for educating handicapped children rests with the local education agencies. This responsibility has been clearly delegated to such districts by state legislatures, along with the responsibility for the education of the nonhandicapped children of such districts.

19

This responsibility does not alter the fact that, in this day and age, there *are* resources outside of the local district which assist the district in carrying out its responsibility to *all* children. Within the forseeable future, *state aid* will be a way of life for the local districts of this country and, in addition, there are some limited federal dollars available for special programs which more than likely would not be operated without such funds. At the very least, however, the local school district should be prepared to spend at least as much for handicapped children as it does for the nonhandicapped and in facilities which are compatible with the programs operated (not the cast-offs which are so frequently the facilities which just happen to be available).

The actual costs for operating school programs for handicapped children will vary from approximately two to four times the cost of educating the nonhandicapped in regular school programs. The mentally retarded and emotionally disturbed require twice the expenditure and the physically handicapped (orthopedically handicapped, hearing impaired and visually impaired) require about four times the expenditure per pupil as nonhandicapped. These excess costs are incurred primarily because of the differential in class size and in the necessity for additional personnel such as diagnostic staff, social workers and medical staff. Yearly transportation costs are usually a major extra cost item in addition to the classroom costs. Depending upon the geographic nature of the area and the distances children are bussed, such costs may run as high as four to five times the cost of transporting nonhandicapped children. When we consider the necessity for house-to-house pick-up and delivery for many children, as well as the cross-district bussing to get children to central instructional centers, it is easy to see how these costs can skyrocket; yet such transportation is essential to the operation of a program for handicapped children.

There is a variety of plans for channeling outside funding to local school districts. The most common of these plans are:

Excess Cost Plans

Assuming that state aid is available to help local school districts defray the excess costs of providing special education, the following are the two most commonly used schemes:

1. PER PUPIL REIMBURSEMENT. State aid is based on the principle of guaranteeing a local school district a minimum level of support for each child. The aid is calculated based on the numbers of children in attendance or counted in membership on a given day. The corollary of this plan for special education purposes is to count each child in attendance or in membership as two or four memberships. Some states make two counts, the first count being the standard count for all children. The second count comes later in the year and the additional memberships are based on this count. The principle is that the counting should be averaged and that the later count may be more accurate because of the chance to screen children into a program as the year progresses.

Any per child reimbursement scheme has a basic defect which can be detrimental to the children involved. Because the reimbursement is based on the *number* of children involved in a program there can be tremendous pressure placed on the staff involved to fill the class prior to the counting days. There have been instances where children have received the barest of screening before being placed, with the stipulation that the screening and diagnosis will be completed at a later date. It should be evident that the placing of a child in a special school setting is of sufficient gravity that every precaution must be taken to protect the rights and feelings of the children and their parents. There is also an unfortunate tendency to fill classes to the maximum size allowed instead of to the optimum number which the teacher can adequately handle, given the characteristics of the learning problems of the children so placed.

2. PER CLASS REIMBURSEMENT. Assuming that a local school district follows state regulations governing the minimum and maximum number of children allowed in a class, per class reimbursement is based on a flat amount for each approved class or program operated by the local school district. This plan appears to provide the opportunity for a more equitable distribution of excess cost dollars because it does not require a local district to load up a class to obtain the reimbursement which all agree is necessary to operate a satisfactory program of special education.

Most states prepare their budget requests for special education by anticipating the numbers of classes or programs which will be operated by local school districts during the next school year. Local districts must obtain prior approval before initiating a program. It is these approvals which constitute the major source of data for the anticipated number of classes which will have to be supported. Because state budgeting is done so much ahead of the actual operating of a school year, it is possible for classes to be approved after the state budget has been submitted, and in some cases actually aproved by the executive and legislative branches of the government. If this happens, or if the amount asked for is reduced by the budget office or the legislature, there would obviously not be enough money available to reimburse each local district the total amount it had anticipated, based on the formula in affect at the time. In this case, money is allocated to local districts on a prorata formula. Michigan, for example, has not paid the full amount in recent memory with the prorata amount being as low as 60 percent at one point. Obviously, the local district must look to other sources for financial support if it does not have the resources at the local level, and this is usually the case.

Florida has a plan whereby the state department of education allocates a set number of classes of various types to local school districts based on the state appropriation in a given year. A local district can count on this reimbursement, but if it wishes to operate additional classes it must do so without any excess cost reimbursement.

3. ADDITIONAL REIMBURSEMENT SOURCES. Some states (such as Michigan and Wisconsin) have a level of school administration between the local district and the state. These units have taxing powers and through use of this taxing authority are frequently able to make it possible for a local district to operate special education programs at no cost to the local school district. This is done by the intermediate unit making up the difference between what a program costs the local district and the amount of state aid which has been made available to the local district. This plan has been a bonanza to many special education programs, but many of these intermediate districts are currently

having difficulty in levying enough taxes to make up the difference. This is particularly true in states where mandatory laws
have been recently enacted. In this case, the local districts are
faced with the decision of whether to put local funds into the
program or to close the program (or never to initiate it).

Federal Aid for Special Education

Under certain conditions, federal money is available to provide some aspect of special education. A basic principle of
federal funding is that the federal dollars cannot be used to fund
programs which have been in operation prior to obtaining the
federal money. Titles I, III, VI of the Elementary and Secondary Education Act (ESEA) can, under certain conditions,
be used for special education purposes. Any school which quali-
fies for Title I money may operate some special education with
this money. The close relationship between cultural deprivation
and mental retardation makes it imperative that each school
district which anticipates operating such programs carefully plan
the relationship of these two educational programs. Title III
has 15 percent of the money appropriated set aside for use in
operating exemplary or innovative programs of special education.
Guidelines and applications are available from state departments
of education. Some of the most highly respected projects funded
under the provisions of Title III have been in the special education area.

Title VI of ESEA was specifically added to the Act to provide
local districts, operating through the states, with the opportunity
to supplement state and local funds for special education. Money
is allocated to each state, which in turn must provide the U.S.
Office of Education, Bureau for Education of the Handicapped,
with a state plan. The plan must have been developed in concert
with local school personnel. Local districts may make application
to the state for money for projects which are included in the
state plan. Guidelines and application for participation in Title
VI are available for state departments of education.

A source of federal funding which is frequently neglected by
all levels of school administration is found in the Vocational

Education Act amendments of 1968. Because of the neglect of handicapped students in most vocational education programs, Congress mandated that 10 percent of the money which was appropriated be spent for handicapped pupils (and 15% for the disadvantaged). Here again, the relationship between mental retardation and cultural deprivation cannot be ignored in planning for the use of these funds. Congress will undoubtedly be calling school administrators and boards of education to account for the expenditure of these funds as pressure grows to expand the offerings in the vocational and technical education area.

Finally, the day is long past when special education can or should depend on handouts from local service organizations for the initiation and support of programs. Such support can continue to provide some "window dressing," but they cannot be considered a mainstay of support. Local superintendents of schools, in consultation with special education personnel, must systematically plan for the adequate financing of special education programs just as they plan for any other part of the educational endeavor before it can attain the level of service which is necessary to meet the educational objectives set for the program.

CHAPTER FOUR

INITIATION AND IMPROVEMENT
OF PROGRAMS—
GENERAL INFORMATION

T HIS CHAPTER AND the next will examine the many administrative conditions and decisions which must be made in operating a program of special education in a modern school. This specific chapter deals with general information which might better be called *auxiliary information* because the specific disability areas will not be discussed. The topic of specific disability areas will be discussed in the next chapter.

An examination of the topical headlines in this chapter will reveal that the topics are discussed independently. It must be remembered, however, that these topics are not mutually exclusive and that they do depend one upon the other. Judicious consideration of each of the topics is essential as administrative decisions are reached.

ADMINISTRATIVE STRUCTURE

Federal Level

Until the time of the 88th Congress the position of programs for the handicapped in the United States Office of Education (USOE) was almost insignificant. The USOE, in spite of many reorganizations, still is structured in the following hierarchy: (1) The Commissioner and his staff, (2) Bureaus, headed by Associate Commissioners, (3) Divisions, headed by Directors, (4) Sections, headed by Section Chiefs, and (5) Units, usually without headship designation. For many years the programs for the handicapped, which at that point were largely data-collecting in nature, were placed at the section level; however, during the 88th Congress, which passed some significant special education legislation, the status of the programs was elevated to a division. After one year of operation, however, the division was dissolved and the component parts were dispersed throughout other units in the USOE in one of the reorganizations which take place periodically. This dissolution was viewed with great alarm by professional special educators, parents and friends, and particularly friends in Congress. The result was that Congress created a mandated Bureau for Education of the Handicapped which pulled together all of the constituent elements which had been in the Division prior to 1965. This Bureau cannot be dissolved without Congressional action and it is the only bureau so mandated in the USOE.

Within the Bureau for the Education of the Handicapped (BEH) there are several divisions: one dealing with state programs, one with the training of personnel, one with educational media for the handicapped, and one with research. The legislating of this Bureau illustrates dramatically the impact of a powerful lobby on the actions of Congress, because it is unusual for Congress to become involved in what is by tradition an executive matter.

It is through this Bureau that federal funds for all special school programs for the handicapped flow with the exception of some funds from the Social and Rehabilitation Services Agency. The SRA is one of the component agencies of the Department of Health, Education and Welfare, as is the USOE. These funds support vocational rehabilitation programs. (More will be said about vocational rehabilitation later.) It must be pointed out, however, that almost every group in the USOE that has funds for expenditure has some opportunities for the handicapped and any director or administrator must be constantly alert as to what these opportunities are. An excellent source of information is the journal, *Exceptional Children,* published by the Council for Exceptional Children, Jefferson Plaza, Suite 900, 1411 South

Jefferson Davis Highway, Arlington, Va., 22202. Periodically this journal, which deals only with programs for the handicapped, publishes an update on federal legislation and its impact and opportunities for the handicapped.

State Level

Educators have more immediate involvement with state departments of education. The states vary, of course, as to where special education is located administratively in the overall administrative structure. In recent years, however, special education has moved up the administrative ladder of state departments just as they have in the federal establishment. Traditionally, there is a director and a series of program specialists whose responsibility it is to work with local school districts, but realistically, they often play the role of "approver of funds." A limited number of people at the state level obviously cannot provide the details of program initiation and improvement which are essential for the operation of excellent programs. Even the approval process by which funds are distributed to local schools is largely *pro forma* because the information on which decisions are made comes from forms which are filled out by the local districts. This is regrettable, but realistic when one considers the thousands of programs which may be in operation in a given state and the limited personnel in most state departments of education even with federal assistance in employment of program specialists.

Cooperative Arrangements

Coming closer to the local level, there are a series of cooperative arrangements in some of our states which allow for different degrees of coordination across local districts. Some of the most common of these will be discussed as follows:

Michigan—Intermediate School District

Early in the 1950's, under the impetus of Dr. William Emerson, Superintendent of the Oakland County Schools, legislation was passed (Public Act 18) which stated that counties of the first class, of which there were only two, could organize themselves to provide supplementary services for the handicapped and at the same time allow the county superintendents of schools to take to the voters of the counties the proposition which would provide a special tax for the handicapped spread over the whole county. These funds would then be disbursed to local school districts to make up the difference between what the programs actually were costing and what state reimbursement would provide. In essence, a special education program would cost a local school district little or no cash outflow. Later in the 1950's the act was expanded so that all counties in the state could participate in this program and at the present time, all counties in the state are a part of an intermediate school district. Since that time the duties and responsibilities of the intermediate school districts have been expanded and include the opportunity for operating programs directly.

Initially this cooperative arrangement provided more than adequate money to operate programs. However, in recent years the tax which was initially authorized has proven to be inadequate to meet increasing demands. Therefore, these intermediate districts have had to return to the voters for increased authorization and are facing many of the same elements of voter resistance as local districts with the resultant curtailment of programs in local districts which cannot operate them without such assistance.

In addition to providing financial assistance, the intermediate districts provide varying degrees of expert help to local districts as they plan programs. Directors of Special Education and program specialists are hired and are made available to local districts. Where local districts have their own director of special education there is the possibility of conflict in philosophy and by definition, the local district takes precedence over the intermediate district in making decisions affecting local districts. Although many fine things have been done in the name of intermediate districts, there is the possibility of administrative conflict and breakdown between the two levels of authority and responsibility.

Illinois Cooperative Programs

Illinois uses an arrangement whereby a series of contiguous local school districts band together to form what are called *cooperative special education programs.* One of the districts serves as the fiscal agent and the superintendents of all districts serve as a board of directors to operate the cooperative agreement. The director and any program specialists that may be employed work for the cooperative agreement and their role is to work with local districts in organizing programs and arranging "swaps" of children and physical facilities. Here again, many fine things have been done for handicapped children, but the hazard still remains that any individual district may not wish to give up any of its sovereignty by refusing in some instances to cooperate for the mutual benefit of the group. This becomes particularly true when physical space in the schools becomes tight or in cases where children have to be transported across district lines (and they usually are) or when money gets tight, as it is at the present time.

SESA Districts

Wisconsin has been divided into special education service areas with functions very similar to Michigan's intermediate districts. However, the districts are much larger and the major concern is the development of cooperation across traditional county lines as well as within and between local districts. Most of the pros and cons of the intermediate or cooperative arrangements are apropos here.

Special School District—St. Louis County, Missouri

A most unique administrative arrangement was started in St. Louis County, Missouri in 1957 when the legislature of the state of Missouri authorized the people of the county to create a special school district to serve handicapped children. This was voted on and approved by the people, along with a tax to support special education programs. Very briefly, the total county was looked on as a special school district for handicapped children although there were over thirty school districts in the

county. In essence, every child lived in two school districts, both
the local and the special district. Thus, for special education
purposes, there were no boundary lines within the county and
children could be moved across local district boundary lines
with no problems of tuition payment or transportation authority,
etc. Testimony to the effectiveness of this arrangement was that,
prior to 1958, fewer than 20 percent of the handicapped children
in the county were being served, while in 1962, this figure was
over 90 percent. In fact, every child who was eligible under
the state laws in existence at that time and whose parents
desired service for him was receiving special education.

There were many visitors to that program from other states
and countries; however, no other unit such as this is in operation
in the United States. In recent years vocational education has
been added to the responsibilities of the Special District and a
similar record of achievement has emerged.

There are other instances of cooperative kinds of programs;
however, those mentioned above constitute the major types of
cooperative arrangements which are in operation at the present
time.[1]

Local Level

Most local districts anticipating having a program of special
education will require the services of a director even though
there may be services available through a cooperative arrangement. One of the evidences of commitment to programs for the
handicapped is the placement of the director in the administrative structure of the district. This placement varies from some
who are placed essentially at the principal's level, although he
may not be called that, all the way to an assistant superintendent
for special education. It has been the author's experience that
the lower the director is placed in the "pecking order," the
less effective he will be in implementing a good program of
special education. Many good directors have left the position
because of the frustration they have felt in not being able to
have access to the superintendent or report through the superintendent directly to the board of education. Good professional
judgments can get garbled in their transmission from someone

at a low level to the ultimate policy making groups. What is being said probably applies to other facets of the school program as well; however, the director of special education speaks for a minimum of 10 percent of the school population, all with special needs, and this would seem to warrant a place in the administrative structure commensurate with the responsibilities.

DIAGNOSIS AND PLACEMENT

The stereotype of testing for placement in special classes is some person moving around from school to school with a Binet kit giving "IQ tests" and on the basis of a test(s), plus school records, recommending that a child be placed in a special class, maintained in a regular class, or worse, being excluded from school.* Fortunately, in recent years there has been much furor over the use and abuse of intelligence tests and the reliance on a given score has come into greater and greater disfavor. Unfortunately, there are all too many states who have offered little protection for students from semitrained individuals, with the result that a person having had a single course in individual intelligence testing can legally certify students as being eligible for classes for the mentally retarded. In 1952, Dr. T. Ernest Newland[2] wrote a penetrating analysis on the difference between *testing* and *assessment*. Obviously, testing is a part of the assessment process, but dealing with the qualitative aspect of objective information is the difference between what makes a person who is a "tester" and one who is a true diagnostician.

The genius of special education is the blend of the various disciplines and skills of medicine, psychology, social work, and education and the ultimate evidence of this blend is in the process for arriving at a proper diagnosis and school placement.

The following specialities are called for in preparing a plan for diagnosis:

1. MEDICAL. Ideally, the services of all medical specialities should be available to school personnel in collecting information

---

* The term itself is incongruous because IQ stands for *intelligence quotient* and that is something which is derived from an intelligence test, thus there is no such thing as an Intelligence Quotient test.

about a given child. From a practical point of view the services of a peditrician, orthopedist, and psychiatrist are those which are most commonly used. The role of the pediatrician is to evaluate all pertinent medical data submitted by the family physicians or other medical sources and to solicit other medical information from these sources. No child should be placed in a special class, regardless of his disability, without having a complete medical workup. All too frequently what are considered by the unsophisticated as educational problems turn out to be medical problems, and as a matter of fact, if medical problems go untreated they frequently are manifested as educational problems.

2. PSYCHOLOGICAL. The services of one or more qualified school psychologists are necessary. It is usually considered that there are three levels of psychological expertise. The lowest level being a *psychometrist* (the person mentioned in the preceeding paragraphs as the "tester"), with the second level being a *psychological examiner,* and the highest level being a *school psychologist.* These are usually people who are trained at the Ph.D. level in the administering and interpreting of instruments designed to collect information about a child's level of intellectual functioning.

3. SOCIAL. The social backgrounds of the children and their families are essential in evaluating the impact of the child's environment on his learning ability or disabilty. Generally speaking, psychiatric social workers are most highly skilled in collecting and analyzing this kind of information.

4. EDUCATION. Someone must be designated as the collector of educational information, both from the previous school history and from tests which are designed to collect information about level of achievement and specific learning skills or disabilities.

5. ADDITIONAL INFORMATION. The services of an audiologist or speech and hearing clinician who is highly trained will be necessary to collect information on hearing loss and/or speech problems and in addition one person must be designated as the individual to test vision. Frequently this can be done through the school nurse if it is not part of the routine medical examination.

The primary function of this section is not to indicate so much who should be collecting information but what types should be collected and by the specialist who is usually most competent to not only collect but to analyze it.

The need for adequate diagnostic information has long been recognized, but the schools most frequently have difficulty in providing a delivery system. The schools create or encourage diagnostic shoppers if they do not provide a complete diagnostic service. For example, if the school provides the psychological service but insists that the parents get the medical examination in one spot, audiological examination in another and some social agency collects the social information, the parents are forced to go from one agency to another and all too frequently they get conflicting advice or recommendations from the various agencies. One child in the author's acquaintance was variously diagnosed as schizophrenic, brain-injured and mentally retarded by three different agencies. In current terminology he would have been classified as having a learning disability and required very specific types of instructional techniques.

One of the efficiencies of cooperative arrangements is that it makes possible the support of an efficient, all-inclusive delivery system for diagnosis and placement activities. Small local districts obviously cannot maintain the complete services of medical, psychological, social and educational nature; however, when they combine their efforts with other districts such services can be solicited and supported. The United States Office of Education has supported some traveling clinics whereby these services are collected in a mobile unit and taken to children in sparsely populated areas.

Let us assume that a child has been referred for possible special class placement in a situation where a well-designed child evaluation center is in operation. Upon receipt of the referral, which should include baseline information, such as the child's name, address, age, brief school history and reason for referral stated in behavioral terms, the referral is reviewed by the school psychologist who will then go to the school for some preliminary checks on the child. This may include some screening tests and some discussion with the child's teacher and principal to determine whether the referral was in truth within the broad guidelines of special education potential. If that visit confirms the referral, the school social worker then submits to the parents a part of a form which will eventually be the social history. The first portion, which is completed by the parents and is returned to the social worker or is brought in on the day of the clinic visit, gives information about the child's home life, i.e. the number of siblings, father's occupation, birth history, developmental history and other items of general nature. At this point the child is scheduled for a visit to the evaluation center along with his parents. Ideally, this should take place within two weeks of the receipt of the initial referral (one of the chief complaints of parents is the length of time it takes to have the children seen in clinics of various sorts, particularly those which cater to children and have large case loads).

On the day of the child's arrival with his parents at the center, the parents are seen by the social worker who completes the social history. The child is then seen by the physician, the psychologist, the educator, and the speech and hearing specialist (with particular emphasis on audiological examination). While the child is still at the center, the information which has been collected is reviewed by each specialist who saw the child or parent during a staffing of the child and an initial decision is made to either reject the child from the program as being ineligible, to accept him in the program, or to recommend that additional information be obtained from either the clinic staff or from outside sources. Once this determination has been made, the two people who seem to have the best rapport with the parents will relay and interpret this information to them with the basic principle being that no parent should leave the clinic day without having had some positive reaction to the information which was collected during that day. Ideally, placement can be decided before the child leaves, and in some instances transportation arrangements can be made.

Before the day is over each specialist will have dictated his report on each child seen and on the next day these reports will be typed so that copies can be sent to the sending and the receiving schools, if appropriate, and one placed in the general clinic file. Placement should be completed as rapidly as possible after the reports have been received, assuming the parent is in agreement that such placement is desirable for his child.

The whole process from referral to placement should be accomplished within a period of not more than one month. All too often placements take three to six months to accomplish. This often leads to the waste of the larger portion of a school year. Naturally, the more complicated the diagnosis, the longer it takes to get all the information. For example, if the child is orthopedically handicapped it will be necessary for him to be seen by an orthopedist, if one is not part of the clinic staff on a regular basis. There may be other medical specialities which will have to be consulted and this, of course, takes additional time. It is with cases of this nature that the director must rely on his medical staff to "bird dog" the case to make sure the information is collected as rapidly as possible from the medical profession.

No child should be placed without the type of evaluation which has been described above. In addition, no child should be moved from one level of a program to another or between programs or be excluded from a program until a complete re-evaluation has been effected. Teachers should have the option to refer children for reevaluation once they have been placed in a special education program, because if special education is effective, the diagnosis may well change and with it the appropriate placement. All placements should be considered tentative, although one may be reasonably sure that the preliminary judgment was accurate. If there is serious question about the placement, a recommendation should be made for a trial placement with some reevaluation at the end of the trial period. This trial might be for as little as two weeks, to two months, to a year. Naturally, in reevaluation not all data will have to be redone, but certainly those data which appear to be changing would need to be updated.

When children are seen by the clinic staff, the referring person should be included in the staffing procedure, so that if a child is not accepted in special education, the regular class personnel can have the benefit of the professional thinking of the evaluation team. As more and more children are being reassigned to regular classes and being kept in regular classes rather than being assigned to special classes, this liaison with the general education program becomes more essential and should be built into any diagnostic and evaluation scheme.

TRANSPORTATION

In most situations, whether they be rural or urban, without special transportation arrangements there would be no comprehensive programs for the handicapped. This does not mean that all handicapped children must ride special busses. In fact, riding regular busses is to be encouraged whenever the child is physically or mentally able to cope with the situation on a given bus. The following suggestions are given to assist primarily in planning special transportation, although in some instances, the regular bus can profit from some modifications. First of all, the busses should not be so large that the director of transportation feels compelled to fill the bus and thus keep the children on far too long. Ideally, routes should be planned so that the time from pick-up to school arrival is not more than forty-five minutes. If the choice is between a longer bus ride and not going to school, most parents and the children would opt for having a longer ride. Even though it would be more expensive to operate many small busses rather than a few larger ones, the small busses will generally produce better public relations and better results.

The following items of equipment are essential in any busses carrying handicapped children and particularly those who would fall into the classification of crippled.

a. *Seat belts for each child and harnesses for given children if necessary.* The harnesses are especially necessary for those who have musculature problems which would prevent them from being able to control the movements of their bodies while the bus is rounding curves, making stops and starts.

b. *Where necessary, the seats at the rear of the bus should be removed (or near the exit which will be used by individuals in wheelchairs) and equipment installed which will clamp the wheelchairs to the wall of the bus.* It is still possible to find clamps which held the hoods of cars down in the earlier days of the automobile industry. These clamps mounted on flexible brackets on the walls of the bus make excellent devices to hold wheelchairs secure so that those children who cannot be transferred to a regular seat can ride in safety. It should be remembered, however, that if a child is riding in a bus in his chair he should also have a seat belt attaching him to his chair or to the wall of the bus.

c. *On thirty-six-passenger busses it is possible to install a hydraulic lift which operates in conjunction with a side door.* Some attempts have been made to install the lift at the rear of the bus; however, this exposes the children to oncoming traffic in a most unprotected position. On smaller busses it generally is not possible to use a hydraulic lift because of the number of seats it removes from use. In such cases ramps can be fashioned which store under the floor of the bus. These are not standard items which are available from bus body companies and would have to be fashioned at a local body shop, probably one that makes modifications for trucks.

d. *The entry doors of the bus should be designed so that both of the doors open outward and the inside of the door should be equipped with assist bars.* The type of bus door that has one door opening in and one out eliminates the possibility of having the two assist bars and also allows for the possibility of children who are not extremely steady on their feet to become dirty in entering the bus as they rub against the door.

e. *The drop-off point at the school(s) should be designed so that the busses can be exited through the rear door.* This is usually designed into new buildings being built to house handicapped children. Such an arrangement reduces the unloading time by 50 to 75 percent and particularly when dealing with children in wheelchairs and those using crutches.

Most handicapped children will require a house-to-house pickup and delivery. For some children it is physically impossible to move to a central pick-up point and for others, especially those who are deaf or blind, the safety factor is such that they should not move long distances unescorted. Essentially, the same is true for the more severely retarded children. The exceptions to house-to-house pick-up and delivery are those children classified as higher level retarded or less severely emotionally disturbed. These children can, and in many cases should, walk to school or walk to a central pick-up point just as any normal child. As indicated earlier, whenever possible, handicapped children should be riding regular school busses where this is the normal pattern for getting to school. There are some problems attendant upon either plan. Where less severely handicapped children are transported with the more severely handicapped, they develop some feelings about their own image. This is particularly true about the higher level retarded children (whose true problem may well be cultural disadvantage rather than retardation). Like all other aspects of school planning, there can be no blanket statement as to what is best for handicapped children. Rather, the principle of examining each handicapped child's needs should also apply to the provision of transportation.

A word about other forms of transportation seems to be in order. Some districts will use taxicabs and station wagons to haul their handicapped children. These may be satisfactory for some types of children, but for those who are physically handicapped (particularly the crippled) these vehicles are not equipped to encourage independence on the part of the children and indeed require considerable physical stamina on the part of the driver to be able to manage the transfer from wheelchair to vehicle to wheelchair.

In sparsely populated areas, some consideration should be given to the use of air transportation for moving the children to selected points. A small helicopter would appear to be an ideal craft for such transportation, although air transportation has the additional hazard of weather problems not usually a factor on the ground. One wonders why individuals in the adjacent forty-eight states are so reluctant to experiment with air transportation, when in Alaska the small helicopter is widely accepted as a means of transportation. Is it cost alone that keeps us from experimenting with such innovations?

TEACHER SELECTION AND RETENTION

Teacher selection has been inordinately influenced in the last decade by the rapidly increasing demand for teachers of the handicapped and the inadequate supply which has prevailed during this period. It has been estimated by the United States Office of Education that approximately 50,000 teachers are currently working with children having handicapping conditions while there is need for over 300,000 if the country were to provide full service to all its handicapped children. The picture, however, is spotty. Some states have more nearly met the need while others are still struggling to attract teachers. Within the field of special education itself, there are areas in which the demand is very extreme, for example, the blind and the deaf. In these two areas there are about twelve requests for every teacher trained. In some other areas, most notably speech pathology, the supply is rapidly approaching the demand. No one has yet been able to adequately assess the numbers of professionals needed to work in the area of learning disabilities. One of the hazards of estimating the number of new teachers needed is the large number of teachers who leave the field for a variety of reasons, some of which will be discussed in later paragraphs. For example, in one of the last years of the federally supported training programs for the deaf, during one year while about 500 teachers were receiving support, almost 500 were leaving the field with a net gain of zero in that year. Obviously, one must examine the administrative and program practices when such a mortality rate occurs.

There has been much controversy over whether or not teachers of the handicapped should receive a higher salary with the same training as a regular class teacher. The author feels strongly that a single salary schedule is imperative, that is, like salary for like training and responsibility. The hazard of paying a bonus or differential is that the nonspecial teachers will resent the special teachers and thus the degree of cooperation which is so essential to the operation of an effective program will be lost on a nonprogram issue.

There have been some interesting developments in teacher training programs, some stemming from a lack of numbers and others from a lack of quality in existing programs. One of the former is a project which was initiated in Aiken County, South Carolina in 1967 under the impetus of an Educational Professions Development Act grant. The constituent school districts of Aiken County employed two teachers for each special class which they anticipated opening in the fall. These were teachers who were certified but untrained in the field of special education. The County opened an experimental or demonstration school and, in cooperation with the University of South Carolina, offered a six-week summer training program for all fifty teachers. In the fall, twenty-five of the teachers went to the schools and opened the classes while the other twenty-five remained with the demonstration school. At the end of the first semester the groups rotated, and at the end of the year both groups were back at the demonstration school for additional demonstration and academic work. The result was that within the period of two summers and one school year fifty teachers were fully approved to work. The project just about doubled the supply of teachers available in the local districts of the county.

The Council for Exceptional Children has long been concerned about the quality of education of teachers and has held several national conferences on the topic of professional education. This activity has stimulated some members of the Council to action. Most of these concerns dealt with competency-based teacher training programs rather than those based on course completion. Dr. Louis Schwartz, writing in the journal, *Exceptional Children*, presented a model for teacher training which was competency based.[3] More recently, the State Board of Education in Michigan has been examining a report from a committee which has designed and recommended a competency-based approval program for all teachers of the handicapped (Morvin A. Wirtz, Chairman of the Committee). The model consists of a core or two thirds of the work which is interdisciplinary in nature and would be required of all teachers. Each of the specialty areas has a smaller share of the overall time block, that is, approximately one third of the time available for the training program. It is significant to note that the requirements are spelled out in behavioral or skill terms with the college or university having to prove or demonstrate that it is conducting a program which will develop or measure these required competencies. This trend is in keeping with the general direction of the state and with the concern of many educators throughout the United States.

All too often in recent years, every teacher could get a temporary approval to teach special education in the year in which she was hired. Frequently these were merely warm bodies occupying classrooms. Many of them were rejects from regular programs who were being assigned to special classes, but particularly in the area of the mentally retarded, in the hopes that the smaller pupil/teacher ratio would make it possible for them to survive for the few remaining days they had until retirement. This type of decision is no longer tolerable in the public schools. The parents are organizing and demanding a higher quality of service and the teacher training institutions are more and more refusing to become involved in such a conversion process, with both decisions being based on the demand for improved services to handicapped children.

It is absolutely essential that every teacher employed to work with handicapped children be interviewed, preferrably after the interviewer has had an opportunity to review the placement credentials. Too often credentials are misleading and one must develop the skill of deciding what to ignore and what to look for that has not been said, as well as what has been said. The credentials will usually give a general viewpoint of a person's competency if there are reports from critic teachers and others who are familiar with his work in the classroom. The interview should concentrate then on the philosophic base on which the person operates to determine whether or not it is compatible with the philosophic base of the employing establishment. One can also press further on the application of competency to hypothetical situations. The author feels that teachers should not be employed who do not have a sound philosophic base on which to operate. Too many teachers might be known as *cookbook* teachers. In other words, they have a page in the book for each type of behavior and they cannot make a decision until they check the recipe. Every teacher should be well grounded in theories of learning which apply to all teaching situations and make educational decisions based on learning theory and knowledge of human development. It is exceedingly important to try to determine the motivation of the individual who wishes to work with handicapped children. The job market is such today that too many individuals are attempting to get into special education—as opposed to regular education—because they feel there is an opportunity for a job. One would hope that these teachers would at least have achieved an approximation of Samuel Laycock's third level of acceptance of handicapped children. Of course, as the competition for training spots becomes more acute, the colleges and universities will be doing a better job of screening out the unfit or improperly motivated before the hiring official ever sees the candidate. One should also be conscious of the mix of experienced and new staff members. If one is in an area in which the teaching staff is relatively stable, recruiting should be done with recently graduated individuals. However, if one is establishing a new program where none previously existed, an attempt should be made to find staff members who have had experience and to mix them with new staff so that there can be a blend between the experience of a veteran and the freshness and creativity of the newly trained.

It was mentioned earlier that all too many of our teachers leave the field of special education after several years of teaching. Many of them are disillusioned about teaching, not because of their own inadequacies but because of inadequacies within the school system. These are the ones toward which we need to direct some attention.

First of all, good supervision and assistance, particularly during the first two years, is absolutely essential in helping the new teachers get their feet on the ground so that they can build a base for future success. The more successful districts employ supervisors to work with first-year people exclusively so that they are available within a very short period of time when the new teacher needs help desperately.

Another factor which contributes to the retention of teachers is properly screened and placed children. If the teacher feels he is being asked to conduct a program for children with whom he has had no training or who are improperly placed in his class, he will become discouraged and may well leave. Some of the newer training programs are broadening the perspective of teachers and will eventually reduce some of this anxiety. Realistically, however, teachers are still trained, by and large, in categorical fashion.

An important factor in retaining teachers is for them to have a chance for their own professional improvement. The district might well develop a professional library which is available to the teachers. They should be encouraged to attend state and national professional meetings. A good policy in this, to assure teacher attendance at a national meeting once every four years, is to provide transportation. If a person achieves national office or is invited to present a paper or participate in the program, however, all expenses should be paid. This public exposure is an excellent recruiting device and will pay for itself many times by attracting teachers to the district. Still another factor is the provision of adequate, teacher inspired and planned, in-service training. Too much in-service training is merely a group of teachers being lectured "at" by some outside expert. The lecture is promptly forgotten and the teachers go back to what they were doing before the lecture. If, however, the teachers become emotionally involved in planning and executing the in-service program, the lessons taught will not be so easily dismissed. It might be well to remember that the principles of teaching children in classes also apply to in-service training of teachers and, in fact, serve as models of the most modern methodology and content.

SELECTION OF DIRECTORS AND SUPERVISORS

Persons selected to serve in the capacity of director or supervisor of special education should be screened very carefully to determine, first of all, the fact that they do have a philosophy of special education and its relationship to the general education program and also to determine just what that philosophy might be. Following this they should have a very definite plan of action as to how they would organize a program to achieve the program goals they have set based on their philosophy. All too often persons aspiring to these positions are content to only continue what they have experienced in their own classrooms without taking into account the broader perspective of special education and its relationship to the general education program. Some states are currently offering a special approval for directors and supervisors and obviously, the person to be employed must meet these minimum qualifications.

The person who serves as a director certainly should be certified to teach in more than one area of the handicapped, in spite of the fact that regulations call for certification in only one area. All too often if a person is trained in only one area, the program reflects his own training and other areas in which he is not as knowledgeable tend to suffer from lack of leadership. He should also have some specific training in the techniques of administration, both in the general sense and in the specific administration of special education. In addition, this person should have at *least* three years of teaching experience.

For some unexplained reason, many persons with a background in psychology gravitate to the administrative positions. Perhaps it is because of their broader exposure to the community through the itinerant nature of the job of psychology. The field of psychology, however, is not an adequate background to direct the program of teaching of handicapped children and for this reason the emphasis on selecting persons should be on their teaching background rather than a background in the area of psychology. This does not mean to say that training and even certification in psychology is not good background, but it should not be the *major* background of the person working as a director.

An attempt should be made to determine the flexibility of the director candidates. Anyone who is locked into a given delivery system would rapidly become out of date unless he has the ability to adapt to a fluid situation. There is also the danger of running the district into an educational deadend. His major concern should be with the development of program and modification of existing programs in keeping with new trends. The person's ability to conceptualize and to develop new educational constructs is of primary importance. He should also have proven his ability to communicate and to work with people. Obviously, the success of a given program is dependent upon the catalytic effect the director has on the people working with him. He is much like an organ player who has to know when to depress the soft pedal and when to open the organ up to full capacity to achieve the desired effect.

Many of the things said about the director will also hold true for the supervisor, although the background need not be as rigorous in terms of breadth of training and experience. Certainly, whoever works as a supervisor should have full certification and a minimum of three years teaching experience in the area in which he intends to supervise. Actually, having training in more than one area is helpful so that the interrelationships between the integral parts of special education can be utilized to the fullest extent for the children in the programs which he will be supervising. Potential supervisors should also have proven their ability to work with people. All of us can recall individuals who were highly trained from a technical point of view but with whom no one could work because they used their knowledge as an intellectual club to beat other people into submission on program implementation. The ability of a supervisor or director, for that matter, to throw out an idea informally and six months later have the idea come back as a full-blown concept from a person to whom it was thrown out is one of the fringe benefits of working in such a capacity. When this happens, one can be sure that the leadership role is being exercised properly, because when the idea comes back, it is because the person proposing it is emotionally involved in the idea and it will have a far better chance of success than if it were imposed from above.

Above all, in selecting either a director or supervisor, it should be pointed out that the person must be intellectually honest so that those with whom he must work know where he stands. This is why he must have a firm philosophic base to serve as a guide to his own thinking so that he does not follow every educational breeze that blows.

PROGRAM TRENDS

Perhaps this section of program trends has no place in a handbook of administration because of the rather fluid situation in which education finds itself today. However, there do seem to be some trends in special education which are apt to be implemented over a period of time on a national basis which may serve as guides for the thinking of individuals planning programs.

Mainstreaming

There is a current emphasis on returning handicapped children to regular classrooms (*mainstreaming* or *normalization*). It is hard to pick up a journal dealing with the education of handicapped children without reading some article on this topic. This trend has been interpreted by some administrators as a mandate for doing away with special education and placing all handicapped children, regardless of their problem, in regular classes. One should read these articles very carefully because it does not appear that that is what is being said. Rather, what is being emphasized is that decisions should be made about children based upon a broader consideration of the children's problems other than the fact that they are handicapped. In other words, as indicated in the section on diagnosis, each child should be evaluated for his own strengths and needs and placements made on the basis of those strengths and needs. If children are placed in regular classes, this means that there should be a redeployment of special education staff so that the children are not just placed and left without assistance. Historically, this is what caused the development of special education and to return to that state of affairs without providing any auxiliary service would soon lead us to the situation where demands for special education will be reinstituted. Where children are returned to regular classes, the best of the special education teachers could serve in the capacity as consultants to regular class teachers so that the handicapped can receive the program modification necessary for their survival in regular classes. This will necessitate the employment of broadly trained special education consultants similar to those trained in Michigan for many years as consultants for the physically handicapped or Type C consultants for the mentally handicapped. The education of handicapped children must be viewed as a continuum of services ranging from regular class placement to special class placement to special schools and residential facilities. Without all of these elements, a district could not be said to have a complete program available to its handicapped children.

Redefinition of Mental Retardation

Until recently, there has been general agreement on a definition of mental retardation for school purposes. Court decisions, such as the Skelly-Wright decision in Washington, D.C. and others which have followed, certainly presage a major philosophic change in store for the schools.[4] Of current concern to many special educators working in the area of the mentally retarded is the lack of interest and/or knowledge on the part of general educators as to the implications of such court decisions. This topic will be discussed in greater detail in the section dealing with programs for the mentally retarded.

Learning Disabilities

Many special educators, and in recent years more and more general educators, are becoming concerned with the area of learning disabilities and how to organize school programs for children who seem to fit into this classification. With the estimates of children suffering from this problem running as high as 20 percent of the school population, one must realistically question whether or not this is a special education problem or a problem of general education. Certainly, the techniques which are being espoused as being effective in this area are developmental in nature and appear to be appropriate for the general development of children, particularly in the early stages of their school life. With the increasing emphasis on the individualization of instruction it would appear that the techniques for treating children with learning disabilities might well be incorporated into the general education program, except in those cases where the severity of the problem is such that the children cannot be programmed for adequately in the regular class. This residual should be the province of the special educators and those for whom they program on a regular basis.

Language Development

There is also a current emphasis on the development of language. This problem is related to the redefinition of mental retardation, the development of bilingual programs, and more specifically to the readiness which must be evident before children can succeed in the academically oriented schools. The question is, whose job is it to develop language? Currently, there is competition for this piece of the program between the speech pathologists, the special educators, the remedial reading personnel, and others who consider themselves specialists in the development of language. Questions must be asked about the acquisition of language and the responsibility of the regular class teacher. If one hypothesizes that the success in school is based upon the facility to use the English language, is it not the responsibility of the regular class teacher to see that such language is acquired and further developed so that academic success can be achieved without resorting to the use of outside specialists with the accompanying labeling that goes on?

Speech Correction

There seems to be a changing pattern of speech correction brewing in the schools. Traditionally, the case loads of speech pathologists have been made up largely of individuals with articulation problems stemming from delayed speech development. There is considerable evidence that large numbers of children with such problems will correct their own problems if they are encouraged to do so in an informal way. If one can convince principals, teachers, and parents that it is not necessary to provide speech correction for these children, then the time of the pathologists can be freed up to work with those children who really do need the services of the speech pathologist. With the children having the more severe problems, increasing the frequency of correction from one to three or four times a week can well reduce the overall correction period by as much as 50 percent. Such a change in program, of course, is predicated upon the ability to modify state regulations dealing with case load. States are beginning to lower the case load requirement so that the speech pathologists are not forced to pad their case loads with the self-correcting cases. Therefore, they can spend their time working with the children who need their services on a more intensive basis.

Diagnostic Placements

There seems to be some interest generated in implementing a program of diagnostic placements for children who are initially diagnosed as having school problems. Operationally, this means that one might well eliminate primary classes for educable mentally retarded, emotionally disturbed, learning disabled, or other categories in which the evidence about an impairment is not clearcut. Placement can be made in diagnostic facilities in which the teacher is trained as a *diagnostician* as well as a teacher so that the original diagnosis can be confirmed or modified as a child progresses through the program. The program elements are developmental in nature, with the idea that the children would be moved into more specialized programs as evidence mounts that such would be the proper placement for them. One of the real advantages of such diagnostic placements is that we avoid labeling children early in their school careers on what may be very scanty or contradictory evidence. The author's experience has been that he could obtain parental permission for diagnostic placements much more easily than for placing children in a categorical program with an absolute label of the children after a limited period of observation and testing. This also gives a "handle" with which to work with parents in accepting the problems of children if they are confirmed by the diagnostic placement.

Early Childhood Education

Although special educators have long recognized that early education for the handicapped is absolutely essential for the greatest development of intellectual and physical capacity, very few such programs were in existence until recently. With the advent of mandatory legislation this picture is changing rapidly. As of July, 1975, eleven states have made it legally possible to operate programs for most of their handicapped children from birth. The evidence in the professional literature is overwhelmingly in favor of such programs and shows, in fact, that without such early intervention, handicapped children are doomed to always be in the position of playing "catch-up" in school and that most of them do not catch up, but rather fall further and further behind in academic work. The federal government recognized this fact and one of the amendments to Title VI of the Elementary and Secondary Education Act added an authority to develop early childhood education programs for the handicapped.

PHYSICAL FACILITIES

In 1965 the author published an article in *American Education* entitled "Something for the Special Child." The following is an abridged version of that article. It gives some of the rationale for building plans which the author has executed and recommendations which he has made to others who are planning facilities for the handicapped.

❊   ❊   ❊   ❊

Joe McIntyre was a familiar sight, navigating around Ypsilanti, Michigan in his electric wheelchair. Many a summer noon I would meet him downtown and spend half an hour shooting the breeze with him—Joe carrying on his end of the conversation by pointing out letters on his portable spelling board.

Joe was severely handicapped with cerebral palsy; he could not walk, his speech was unintelligible, and the only part of his body he could use with any degree of sureness was one hand. Yet, because of his own tremendous native ability, he managed to make a living and a life for himself with a little greeting card shop.

When he was a child it didn't occur to anyone that Joe should be given an education. It wasn't until he was in his early teens that a special education administrator allowed him to attend school. But the simple problems of getting around the building proved so great that Joe's formal education was given up after less than two years.

Today there are nearly five million handicapped children such as Joe who are missing their opportunity to receive a proper education because there are still no adequate school facilities for them. This fact is doubly tragic, since educators have tried to give special care and training to handicapped youngsters for the past century (the first class was started in 1866). But throughout the years their work was too often shunted into makeshift quarters. I remember one of the classrooms where I taught educable mentally retarded youngsters back in 1946—it was a miserable basement room with rock walls.

School construction takes money; money comes from local and state governments and through public support. Most school boards have to justify their expenditures on the basis of "the greatest good for the greatest number." Consequently, facilities for the relatively few children who need special education are pushed out of the budget.

It takes more than money, however, to provide the handicapped child with the learning environment he needs. It takes careful planning, which means close coordination among architect, educator, administrator, and taxpayer. Too often, handsome school buildings are conceived and constructed without sufficient attention to the needs of exceptional children.

In a community where I once lived, six million dollars was spent on a new high school. The building was to include classrooms for the physically handicapped from that community and, on a tuition basis, from a neighboring community also. When the first handicapped students enrolled, it became evident that the planners should have consulted the special educators about the specific needs of the physically handicapped. This gorgeous, multi-level building had no elevators and no ramps. There were two steps here, three steps there, forming impossible barriers for children in wheelchairs. As a result of this poor planning, many youngsters remained on home instruction—a costly affair.

Even on a short-term basis, the original cost of architectural studies and careful planning quickly pays for itself.

A few enlightened school districts have seen the logic of good planning. In these communities there is an understanding school administration backed up by a sympathetic school board and an enlightened citizenry. Without *all three* of these elements, a district has little hope of providing appropriate school facilities for the handicapped.

It is difficult to persuade citizens to give financial support to these programs. Even though there is growing public awareness of mental retardation and handicapping diseases, few people understand the effect of these conditions on a child's life and educational needs, nor do most people realize the immensity of the problem.

The number of handicapped youngsters eligible for special education has been growing by approximately 80,000 a year. There are varied reasons for the increase. First, medical and psychiatric diagnoses have become more exact, so that many children are today recognized as handicapped who yesterday would have been called "behavior problems." Second, compulsory school attendance laws are bringing out into the open many handicapped children who once would have been hidden away at home. Third, there is a trend toward bringing into regular classroom situations even those children who are very severely handicapped.

Until the last few years many special education people thought of letting only the moderately handicapped attend classes. I discovered a school about ten years ago where the only handicapped children being taught were those who were completely ambulatory—only three or four even used crutches. I asked the teacher and the physical therapist, "Where are the rest of the kids?"

"What other kids?"

I said, "Well, in a school district this size you probably have at least half a dozen cerebral palsied children, and I don't see any of them here in school."

"Oh, they can't go to school," said the teacher. "They're too handicapped."

But more and more of these handicapped youngsters are coming into our schools and this has produced a vital need for adequate architectural planning. Unfortunately, such planning is still very rare.

The fault does not lie solely with the architect. Educators must also share the blame because they have not stated their needs. Surely it is a tragic waste of opportunity for architects to be designing schools without a clear awareness of the problems and needs.

One of the most useful and enlightening attempts made so far to get a dialogue started between architects and educators was made last May by the American Institute of Architects (AIA) in Washington, D.C. Thirty experts in the fields of architecture and special education spent two days discussing the problems and some possible solutions in the design of facilities for educating the handicapped. More questions than answers came out of the workshop, but it was a promising beginning.

Despite a lack of clear guidelines for constructing school facilities for the handicapped, some useful hints can be drawn from the practical experience of special educators.

Basic principles of design are most obvious when providing facilities for the crippled. Mobility and safety are the prime objectives for children who wear cumbersome braces or use walkers, wheelchairs, or crutches. Most of these children are mentally alert and of normal (some above normal) intelligence. They would be at ease in a regular classroom if they could be freed from hazards and barriers such as stairways. Any variations in floor level through-out a building should be ramped. Where there is more than one floor, elevators should be used, and these should be large enough to accommodate a wheelchair.

Doors should be of a forty-eight-inch wide hospital-type with handles rather than knobs. A child who has only partial use of his hands and arms cannot turn a knob but can usually manage to hook his arm over the pull-handle on the hospital-type door and open it. Door closers are available that keep the door open as long as ninety seconds, a blessing of time for a child who must move slowly. Some automatic doors open and close by treadle or electronic eye.

Classrooms should be closer to square-shaped than to the usual rectangular shaped rooms and should be large enough to enable from twelve to fifteen children with bulky equipment to have freedom of movement. The classroom should also have running water, with a drinking fountain placed in the sink in such a way that a child in a wheelchair can get a drink or wash his hands without help. Any under-sink plumbing should be recessed so as not to interfere with the use of a wheelchair.

Chalkboards should be low enough to be reached by a youngster in a wheelchair. Several types of adjustable chalkboards are avail-able. One of these can be brought to within thirty inches of the floor and can be pulled away from the wall on parallel arms and literally placed over the lap of a child in a wheelchair. Hooks and a holding bar enable a youngster to hang his crutches and free one hand for writing on the chalkboard.

A child who is on crutches or confined to a wheelchair obviously cannot use standard toilets. A washroom should be fairly close to the special class or classes used by crippled children. Toilet stools of varying heights should be set off-center in the booths in order to allow enough room for a wheelchair. A canvas curtain should be used instead of swinging doors, making it easier for the youngster to wheel through in a chair. Holding bars should be within reach around wash basins and urinals; wash basins should be set low enough to permit a child in a wheelchair to wash his hands. Provision should be included for changing and tending children whose physical condition makes them incontinent.

Moving long distances—from class-to-class, to the cafeteria, to the library, to the auditorium, or other common areas—is exhausting and time-consuming for most crippled children. Buildings designed with this fact in mind provide outside exits for each classroom and locate special classrooms for convenience to other facilities.

It has been considered traditional to put handrails along the halls of facilities for the physically handicapped. I do not believe handrails are necessary. Once children are trained to use crutches properly, they should use them. But I have seen children come into a school corridor, hang their crutches over their arm, and go shuffling down the hall relying on the railing.

It would be better to eliminate the handrails and widen the corridor by an extra two feet so that children would have room to use their crutches or chairs properly. It should be our intention to help these children to live as normal a life as possible.

At the AIA workshop meeting, Frank Gentile of Abilities, Inc., described his group's new Human Resources School in Nassau County, New York. It is a school for severely physically disabled children of average or above-average intelligence who were previously on homebound instruction or a limited in-school program.

Mr. Gentile explained that there were forty-seven such children in the school last year and there will be 100 this fall ranging from kindergarten to twelfth grade.

The school tries to provide a total academic program and to deemphasize rehabilitation. Health and medical facilities are included only as they would be in any school: a full-time nurse and a visiting doctor. The youngsters are given opportunity for as broad an educational experience as possible, including physical education. "We've built an adapted swimming pool which children in wheelchairs can use. We have a bowling alley. We have an all-purpose gymnasium," Mr. Gentile said. "We have emphasized the fact that these are children, and not that they are disabled."

In some cases a school district's facility needs to be a special school. A special wing may be built onto a regular school. In small school districts, there may be only a handful of youngsters in this category and a need for only one or two special classrooms.

Whether the facility is a special wing or a special school, the commonly used facilities should be located in the special wing of the school. Proximity to the cafeteria or multipurpose room, the cluster of classrooms, or to the therapy room must be carefully worked out. If the children are to be integrated into regular class activities for any purpose, the facility should be put between other kinds of classrooms so that the less mobile of the crippled youngsters do not waste time and energy.

The National Society for Crippled Children and Adults (NSCCA) has been campaigning to eliminate architectural barriers and hazards in all public buildings. The Society's published standards should be consulted by school administrators and architects planning a school, whether it is to be used only by physically handicapped children or by the general public (which may include physically handicapped adults). Eighteen states require that all public buildings be built in accordance with NSCCA standards.

Children with other types of handicaps can also be brought into normal school situations. The largest single group of handicapped children are those with speech difficulties. These youngsters need the part-time services of a speech therapist and a room designed for special instruction.

Youngsters who are hard of hearing can also spend most of the day in regular classes and part of the day in a special facility. Their primary need is for a space where the itinerant staff can work. Too frequently this is "leftover space," such as a converted storage closet in some remote corner of the school plant. But, again, the special room should be centrally located, with enough electrical outlets for audio equipment and storage space for a variety of other equipment and supplies.

Facilities for teaching the deaf also present some distinct design problems. The average classroom is far too large for them, although flexibility in room size can be obtained with folding doors and cabinet partitions. Again, provision must be made for electrical wires and outlets. Facilities for projectors, a screen, and other visual aids should be an integral part of the classroom plan.

Ten percent of all children needing special education are those who are visually handicapped. This category includes both the partially sighted and the totally blind. The trend is toward sending these children into regular classrooms after the careful development of their four remaining senses. More than half the blind children going to public schools are in regular classrooms for some part of their education. Once oriented to the building, most of the blind youngsters can go off in any direction without help. For their safety, however, some precautions need to be taken. Projections (water fountains, fire extinguishers, display cases) should be eliminated from hallways and class aisles. School doors opening into tile can be put on walls, or flooring of a different texture can be some facilities for the blind, although they are not practical for general use.

Perhaps the most serious problem faced by blind and partially sighted children is caused by steps. Although we are training blind children to be more mobile in their school environment, they still depend upon auditory cues for their reaction to the space around them. Added cues can be built in. For example, strips of acoustic tile can be put on walls, or flooring of a different texture can be placed near obstructions.

Since some blind and all partially sighted children can distinguish differences of light and dark, doors and steps could be painted in colors that contrast sharply with surrounding walls.

Blind children in the same classes with normal youngsters do need more space. Braille books and other equipment (typewriters, braille writers, talking books, record players) require extensive space, both in use and in storage. Booths can sometimes be provided so that the blind student may use his individual listening devices or noisy writing equipment without distracting others in the room.

One of the most prevalent handicaps today is mental retardation. This year there are more than a million mentally retarded children needing special instruction.

For higher level educable mentally retarded children, the physical surroundings for learning can be pretty much standard— in fact, this is desirable because the object is to prepare them not only to participate in the general school program but to be accepted by other children. The less they are isolated in a special facility, the better.

For the middle and trainable groups, however, separate facilities appear to be more satisfactory. For middle-group children space should be provided for music and physical education as well as for academic courses. But perhaps more important are facilities for homemaking and occupational readiness. If adequately educated, many of them can eventually hold a job in a sheltered environment.

Trainable mentally retarded children can participate in many of the activities of the middle group. For the younger trainable children, however, some modifications are necessary.

Both the trainable and the middle groups need to be near a play area where they can "let off steam." Much of their training necessarily involves broad physical movements. This calls for classrooms that open directly into an inside or outside play area. Proximity to the play areas is important because the children's attention span is short; their learning activities need to be interspersed with some physical activity, perhaps as often as every 15 or 20 minutes.

At least another 10 percent of all handicapped children are those with major learning disabilities. These children are sometimes known as "brain-injured" or "hyperkinetic." Sometimes they are confused with the emotionally disturbed. They have been called the "children with too many names" because their conditions are difficult to diagnose accurately. There are, in fact, so many variations that each child is a problem.

Certain techniques used in teaching these children present a challenge to the school designer. The major need is to control auditory and visual stimulation; acoustically treating the walls and ceiling, carpeting the floor, opaquing a window, visually shielding one classmate from another.

The most common solution is portable or built-in booths along a wall. This means, however, that the children face the wall and must turn around to communicate with the teacher. A circular arrangement of booths can be more effective. The teacher stands in the center; the children can see the teacher but not each other.

This year 972,000 school-age youngsters have been identified as emotionally disturbed.

Emotionally disturbed children usually have normal intelligence, but cannot get along with other children or with their teachers.

In order to free the teacher and the pupil from the consequences of violent outbreaks, thought must be given to durability and maintenance. I have seen facilities made of destructible material almost ruined in a short time. The concern for maintenance has been carried to the extreme in some places, with chilling ceramic tile on floors and walls. Newer plastic sprays over cinder block give less of a clinical appearance and yet are washable. The architectural challenge is to coordinate practicality of construction and maintenance without elimintaing the warmth and beauty so much needed by disturbed children.

Even with the most skilled teacher, these youngsters can become uncontrollable. A "quiet place" is needed where the unmanageable child can be isolated until he regains control.

A classroom for the emotionally disturbed can be very distracting to other classrooms nearby. The need to isolate these youngsters is, therefore, understandable. However, the question of isolating *all* types of handicapped children from normal children draws heated debate among special educators. One school of thought would integrate all types handicapped children into the general schoolroom atmosphere as much as possible. Another theory maintains that the child will receive the best education in a separate facility.

Integration seems to be the general trend, however. In Pennsylvania, 55 percent of the children who were in residential institutions for the blind and deaf ten years ago are now in public school classes. Of the mentally retarded youngsters in that state, 15 percent are no longer in institutions but have moved into public schools.

Educators are striving to help handicapped youngsters acquire self-sufficiency and social adequacy so that they will grow up to participate as citizens in the community. These goals are reached not only through good teaching but through proper school environment.

Some educators point out that normal children gain experience and understanding by association with handicapped children. Parents of handicapped children also emphasize the need for their youngsters to be with normal children. The answer to the argument probably lies in the need for variety. There must be a broad range of programs fitted to the needs of the groups with common handicaps, with consideration for the geographic distribution of these children. A major problem is bringing together enough children with a common need to justify the expense of building and equipping a facility.

Smaller school districts usually set up a cooperative school and transport youngsters from a wide area to it. But how far can one transport a handicapped child? Most educators believe that a youngster should not spend more than a half hour each way on a school bus. This is not a hard and fast rule; however, in Philadelphia, brain-injured children ride forty miles through congested suburban sections to a special facility southeast of that city. Contrary to the administrators' fears, the children are thriving on the experience. An assistant teacher rides with them and has taught them to sing as they go. They have learned to sit still and pay attention to the outside. The bus ride is actually an extension of their classroom experience.

Except in the large metropolitan areas, however, it may take as much as a two hundred mile radius to find enough children to justify a school in which a variety of special facilities can be provided. For the handicapped child, a normal home environment may be far less important than being put in a situation in which he can be educated, learn to cope with his handicap, and become economically and socially self-sufficient.

The answer may be a residential boarding school. It may be an isolated day school exclusively for the handicapped, or a wing or cluster of classrooms within a regular public school. It may be simply the modification of a normal school building so that crippled children can get around easily. The location and type of school are directed by what is appropriate for the circumstances and the community.

Whatever the facility, the image presented physically should be distinctly that of *school.* It should look like a school and not like a hospital or a library or a country club. Handicapped children have an overriding desire to rise above their handicap, and as much as possible, to be like their brothers and sisters and neighbors. To them, much more than to the normal child, school is an intensely important part of life.

I know of a young girl who for fourteen years was confined to a single room on the second floor of her home because it was too difficult for her parents to get her up and down. For her, the sight of a bus or a car or children playing was a marvel. When we can make it possible for such youngsters to get out of their confinement and into classrooms, we owe them pleasant surroundings.

I have had many an argument over the construction of buildings with windows high in a wall so that children cannot see out. I personally think the stimulation of an outside view as well as the educational possibilities inherent in the outside world far outweigh the distraction a view may cause.

I like to see plants or pictures or other decorative accents in a lobby. An artist gave my old St. Louis Special School District a beautiful terra cotta statue. It was placed on a table and moved from school to school. One of the delights of my life was to watch small crippled children and mentally retarded children come by and touch the statue.

Obviously, that statue was doing something very important for those children. I'm afraid that school planners seldom give these youngsters credit for noticing beauty.

Tragically little has been done to provide the kind of atmosphere, teaching, and facilities handicapped youngsters need. There has been no opportunity for really conclusive research by either the architects or the special educators. Such research is costly and few localities have been able to justify expenditures for it. Thus, the many and frequent theories held by educators are based on scanty evidence.

Situations need to be created in which teaching methods, physical environment, and specific handicapped groups can be put together and studied. Once a solid base of evidence is produced, educators and architects will be in a better position to convince school boards and the community of the scope of the need.

The Council for Exceptional Children, in cooperation with the American Institute of Architects, has succeeded in generating some interest in developing facilities which are adequate for the needs of handicapped children. Although the major emphasis has been

on the elimination of physical barriers, considerable attention has
been given to the effects of the total school environment on the
learning patterns of children. This includes the visual, acoustic, and
tactual aspects of the environment.

❅   ❅   ❅   ❅

Above all else, the major emphasis in designing any facility
for the handicapped must be placed on assisting the handicapped
to lead as independent a life as possible. We cannot develop
the attitude of independence as an adult if the children are kept
in an environmental cocoon during the years in which their attitudes toward themselves and society are being formed.

There is considerable controversy over the types of physical
facilities which should be available to the handicapped, ranging
from those who say that all handicapped should be educated
or treated in separate facilities to those who claim that all handicapped children can be taken care of in regular schools. The
truth probably lies somewhere between these two extreme positions. Certainly, there are some children who need a sheltered
environment, and for those who need it, it is essential that
it be available for them. This might include the more severely
emotionally disturbed, some of the brain-injured (the more
hyperactive), and the more severely mentally retarded. Unless
a variety of facilities are available, a school district cannot
be said to have a complete program. The facilities should be
designed to meet the needs of children, rather than placing
children in facilities which someone "armchairs" as being best
for them. Actually, there has been little research on the effects
of separate facilities for the more severely handicapped. However, the programs which are generally proposed for these more
severely handicappd children seem to indicate that more can
and should be done in a specialized facility than can be done
if the children are placed in a regular classroom in a non-
specialized school. Many regular schools could accomodate
handicapped children if minor modifications were made in them
such as ramps at the front door, elevators, attention to the
lavatory facilities, drinking fountains, door width, and acoustic
treatment at strategic positions. Such minor modifications remove

the necessity of black or white decisions on *all* handicapped children and provide the diagnostic and teaching personnel with some options in making placement recommendations.

A CENSUS—PRO AND CON

In an attempt to get a more accurate count of the needs of handicapped children and the degree to which they are being served, many states have instituted an annual census of handicapped children. Generally, these state census activities leave much to be desired, primarily because the instructions do not clearly spell out the criteria for handicapping conditions. Rather, they rely on the broad umbrella-type definitions which are usually included in the state laws. The author knows from experience that a tremendous amount of effort goes into conducting such a census; therefore, it seems appropriate to look at the pros and cons of this activity.

Pros

If a census is carried on vigorously and with adequate diagnostic staff, the mere fact that one is attempting to identify the handicapped will unearth some children who may well have been missed in a more cursory examination of the school population.

If the census is done with a reasonable degree of accuracy it will provide some basis for making educational plans, particularly the long-range type, even though the usual census will miss many children. Such planning seems more applicable to the state level than to the local level. At the state level, budgets are prepared from one to two years in advance, and the individuals involved are not concerned with the specific needs of a local school district. Instead, they use this information to obtain money from state sources.

Cons

The biggest problem in conducting a census is found in the lack of expertise in planning and executing the census operation.

Without each child actually being diagnosed as being handicapped, many will be included who are only suspects and will be reported as being real cases. In some categories of handicapping conditions, even the suspects will not be reported. For example, in St. Louis County the author discovered one school district that was reporting twelve trainable mentally retarded children, which was reasonably accurate, but reported only sixteen educable retarded children. Anyone knowing anything about the statistics of handicaps knows that there should be approximately ten times more educable mentally retarded than trainable. It can readily be seen that any planning based on inaccurate evidence such as this will lead to gross underplanning in serving the needs of handicapped children. Generally, the numbers of handicapped children will be underreported rather than overreported, except in the area of high-level educable retarded and the children with minimal speech problems. These are the two areas which tend to be overreported.

For planning purposes, a school district could just as easily use the national sampling statistics projected against the total school enrollment. These sampling studies are scientifically defensible and adequately reflect state and local needs. In St. Louis County, after much diagnostic work, it was discovered that incidence rates were within one hundredth of a percent of the commonly accepted sampling study projections. One cannot help but raise the question of why go through the census for planning purposes when other devices are more accurate. If one is talking about actually placing a child in a classroom, this is an entirely different matter from doing the census type sampling.

WORKING WITH PARENTS

It must be remembered at the outset that parents of handicapped children have *problems*. For example, many of them have exhausted the family resources, both financial and emotional, for the handicapped child, and although they will indicate that they have done this of their own free decision, they do develop guilt feelings, particularly if there are other children in the family who have been, or are being, denied some of the niceties of life or perhaps a college education. One of the common items unearthed by social workers is that parents of handicapped children do have guilt feelings and that they are attempting to establish a familial blame for who produced the handicapped child. Even in relatively sophisticated families this is a problem. These people can be worked with if they have the background to understand a simple explanation of recessive genes, birth injury, and items of this nature. In fact, I do not hesitate to assist a family in utilizing the explanation of birth injury rather than allowing the family to get "hung up" on genetic causation unless there is an obvious need for genetic counseling. The parents with whom it is most difficult to work are those who have a fatalistic or "God's will" attitude toward their problems of having a handicapped child. They tend to see the handicapped child in a "Jobian" light and frequently do only the minimum necessary to help the child to develop his potential.

Most parents want to believe that their child will grow out of the problem or overcome it in some way. Many of the children have had only minimal success in other treatment agencies and the parents see the school as a panacea. The result is a series of unrealistic aspirations on the part of the parents for what the school can do for the child and for what the child can achieve in school. They are also unrealistic as to what the child will be like and what he may do as an adult. Most parents have given little thought as to what their children will be doing as adults. Too often, they are aided and abetted by physicians and educators who are either unaware of the real limitations of the child or unwilling to help the parents face reality. The first step in realistic school planning for a handicapped child is to help the parents develop a plan for the child, taking into account his potentialities and limitations. Unfortunately, the parents usually make their plans based on the rare exceptions which are written up in popular magazines and never see the case histories of the children who do not succeed as well as they might like.

Perhaps one of the most important aspects of program development in the United States in recent years has been the development of parent associations. By and large these are truly organizations of parents helping parents. The schools serving handicapped children should capitalize on the existence of these organizations, and if they are not there, should establish some of their own. It must be remembered, however, that as these parent associations become more sophisticated, they lose some of the early impetus of the association which was to give parents an opportunity to explore with other parents their own uniquely personal problems. When the organization reaches the sophisticated level in which its major business is fund raising, political aspects of providing programs and other less personal programs, then much of the usefulness of the organization for helping parents to understand their own problems will be lost.

The major responsibility of the administrator working with parents of handicapped children is to select the right professionals, that is educators, psychologists, social workers, or physicians, or combination thereof, to counsel with the parents. For example, a parent who may have had an unfortunate experience with the family doctor may more easily accept realistic counseling from a psychologist or an educator. Reference is made to this type of interpretation in the section dealing with diagnosis and placement. In any case, the parents must have the opportunity to cathart with someone whom they feel is knowledgeable and interested in their problems, and then to help them pick up the pieces and go on from there. Schools do have the legal authority to force children into school placements for handicapped and on rare occasions this authority should be used. It is usually better, however, to give the parent a chance to see his child in comparison to other nonhandicapped children. A few months, or even a year, out of a child's school life would be well spent if the parents became acutely aware of their child's limitations rather than forcing the child into the special program and having the parents spend the rest of the child's school life being bitter about the school placement.

Because of the way clinics and schools are organized, parents are asked to come to the schools for counseling and school planning. They usually sit on one side of the desk while the director of special education or the superintendent sits on the other side in his position of authority. In many cases, more can be accomplished if the professionals will see the parents on their home ground. When this takes place, the parents are in the superior position and the professionals are in the inferior position. Therefore, the parents are not as threatened, and are usually more amenable to realistic suggestion. When it is necessary to bring parents into an office setting, they should be made as comfortable as possible by using informal seating arrangements. Refreshments appropriate for the occasion may be served, and everyone may engage in some relaxing small talk before getting down to the business at hand.

It is generally advisable to make as few commitments as possible on programs and placement on the basis of a director's or superintendent's office visit with parents. One should, however, commit oneself to a thorough investigation of the reason the parent was there with the promise that something positive will be done or recommended. Generally the parents will appreciate a considered opinion and recommendation rather than one that is made "from the hip."

Schools tend to get into difficulty with parents because they do not keep them informed on program or placement changes. For example, several years ago the city of Kalamazoo, Michigan decided to decentralize its school program for the deaf; that is, scattering the classes into elementary schools with the well-trained teachers of the deaf going with the children, but leaving the comfortable confines of a specialized facility. This plan was announced to the parents shortly before school was to start in the fall and as one might guess, it was not well received by the parents initially. This was the subject of considerable discussion at several board meetings which were rather acrimonious in nature. It is comforting to know that the professional decision was correct and that the classes are functioning very well. However, much of the furor could have been avoided by advanced planning with the parents and in particular getting key parents to interpret to other parents who may not have been as enamoured of the plan.

The best salesmen a good program has are satisfied parents

and, of course, satisfied children. These people should be utilized in selling the program and not only when levies to support the program are anticipated. The author recalls one parent who organized her family to distribute 10,000 handbills in her neighborhood, and in addition talked to every organization in her sphere of influence. She did this as a result of a PTA meeting in which parents were asked to be ambassadors for the program and she took the charge extremely seriously. The administrators of school districts, to be successful, must be aware of such people and organize them in a positive fashion in support of the program.

CURRICULUM DEVELOPMENT AND IMPROVEMENT

The common cliché in discussing curriculum development and improvement is that the only thing that individuals who serve on such committees do is to select textbooks, and that the real curriculum developers are the textbook publishers. A real curriculum committee will not be dominated in its deliberations by "what's on the market." Instead they will examine the needs of children and plan to meet those needs and then begin to look for curriculum support materials. Another thing that a curriculum is *not* is a recipe book. Too many teachers want a guide which tells them what to do in each specific instance. Such people are usually the most inadequately trained and experienced. It should be assumed that teachers have enough background in learning theory and child development to be able to adapt from a guide to a specific situation. In other words, a curriculum is a guide for the instructional process, including content, materials necessary to carry on the instructional program, and the methodology of getting across the activity.

Teachers frequently ask the question of why they should be burdened with the task of developing a new curriculum when there are so many guides which are available from school districts and the state. Certainly, there is a degree of security in using any curriculum which has been tried and which gives some evidence of meeting the needs of a particular group of children. This must be contrasted, however, with the need for adaptation of any guide to the local situation and the excitement which the development of a new or modified curriculum engenders in the individuals involved. As curriculum committees begin to deliberate about their task they should certainly collect existing guides for study and perhaps use them as a springboard for their effort. However, it should be recognized that teachers will become emotionally involved in their own curriculum and therefore it has a better chance of being implemented over one that has been made available from an outside agency or group.

In some ways, the process of developing curriculum is as important as the product which is produced. Ivan Garrison, for many years the Director of Special Education in Jacksonville, Illinois, once stated that his curriculum guides for his special education programs would never be completed and that they were always in draft form. He felt that the ongoing process of revision was one of the most stimulating activities that his staff carried on. This can best be described as a renewal process for staff and administration and, in some instances, for the students involved. In setting up a curriculum committee, the membership should be built on a rotating basis so that as many faculty as possible have an opportunity to be involved. Also, the curriculum for a particular group of children, i.e. mentally handicapped, deaf, etc. should be viewed and constructed as a whole, that is, from preschool through high school so that it "hangs together." In other words, the curriculum should be developed as a package. This is the only way to insure that a program of study which encompasses all of the content and activities to complete an education are included. Obviously, such a large group of staff would be unwieldly for the day by day developmental activities. This phase of the activity can be most efficiently handled by breaking the overall committee into subgroups and having them work on specific levels, either by their own choice or their level of assignment.

One of the most difficult elements of curriculum development is to agree on the major goals of the curriculum. If one views a curriculum as a pyramid, with the apex of the triangle being the *good life,* curriculum development becomes relatively simple because we can begin to identify elements of what constitutes a good life for various groups of children. It will be different for the mentally retarded, the deaf, and any other group when viewed as a whole. In other words, the *good life* is a very personal thing, based on abilities, disabilities, and opportunities and interests. Further down the pyramid would appear the broad goals, that is, goals such as those enunciated by the White House Conference on Children and Youth in 1930, i.e. civic responsibility, self-realization, human interaction, and economic usefulness. The next move down the pyramid is to develop specific objectives to meet the broad goals which contribute to the *good life*. These obviously are an expansion of the items which contribute to a good life and are translated into items such as learning to read and arithmetic skills. The base of the pyramid is the daily activities which are carried on with individual children and the content which is being taught in these activities. Each daily activity should be analyzed to see if it contributes to the *good life* for the group for which it was intended. Any daily activity which contributes to more than one specific objective is better than one which contributes to only one specific objective. That is, one might teach affective skills at the same time and with the same activities as one teaches cognitive skills. This would be a superior activity to one which taught only cognitive skills.

These can be stated in a curriculum guide in a format which indicates the following: long-range goals—specific objectives (competencies)—daily activities—teaching aids—and auxiliary materials.

The most important item is that a curriculum should never be considered *finished*. It is always in a developmental state and should be revised constantly as new types of materials become available and new activities are possible with changing technology. Also, the curriculum must be responsive to the changing philosophy of the schools and the community.

REFERENCES

1. Lord, Francis, and Insberg, Robert: *Cooperative Programs in Special Education.* Council for Exceptional Children, Washington, D.C., 1964, 1-60.

2. Newland, T. Ernest: Are exceptional children assessed or tested? *Except Child, 19*:2, 51-55, Nov. 1952.
3. Schwartz, Louis: An integrated teacher education program for special education—a new approach. *Except Child, 33*:6, 411-417, Feb. 1967.
4. Ross, Sterling; DeYoung, Henry, and Cohen, Julius: Confrontation: Special education and the law. *Except Child, 33*:1, 5-12, Sept. 1971.
5. Wirtz, Morvin: Something for the special child. *American Education, 1*:6, 14-21, Sept. 1965.

CHAPTER FIVE_ _ _ _ _ _ _ _ _ _

INITIATION AND IMPROVEMENT
OF PROGRAMS—
SPECIFIC SUGGESTIONS

━ ━ ━ ━ ━ ━ ━ ━ ━ ━ ━ ━ ━ ━

E ACH OF THE areas of the handicapped is a specialty of its own, and there is a body of knowledge about the daily operation of programs available in the literature. This chapter, however, will attempt to give only a thumbnail sketch of each of the areas, giving some of the basics every administrator should know and use as a guide for the establishment and operation of programs. It must be recognized that programs are constantly being evaluated and changed to conform to current needs and new information.

SPEECH DEFECTIVE

The area of speech correction has undergone, and is undergoing, changes based on current information. For many years the caseloads of speech pathologists were set at unreasonable levels by state regulation. Many of the states required each pathologist to work with 120 children in order to qualify for full state reimbursement. Because of the high caseload requirements, many of the pathologists were loading up their rolls with children who had only minimal speech problems, working with them for only brief periods of time, and then really spending their time with those children who had more severe disabilities. This was dramatically illustrated in St. Louis County in 1962, when the Special School District was required to provide speech correction for the nonpublic schools. In a three-week period all of the nonpublic school children were screened for speech problems and in the first three grades the percentage of children with various problems was almost identical in the public and nonpublic schools, in spite of the fact that correction had been going on in the public schools for many years. The percentages began to change dramatically as the children moved through elementary schools. The noncorrected population showed about 6 percent at sixth and seventh grade level, with the corrected population being down around 1 percent. An analysis of the individual cases showed that many of the children with minimal problems would correct their own speech if left alone. These were the kinds of children with whom the pathologists had been filling their loads at the request of parents, teachers, and administrators. As a result of this survey, the Special District did not give correction to anyone in the first three grades unless the children had problems of the more severe type. Instead, the caseload was reduced and the amount of time given to each child during the week was doubled and in some instances quadrupled. The result was a reduction in the correction time from an average of twenty-two months to twelve months. On a strictly empiric basis, one can only suppose that the correction of the speech problems in a shorter length of time would be better for the children psychologically instead of "stringing out" the correction for two to three years. This philosophy is beginning to find its way into state regulations which are requiring reduced caseloads as a result of this survey and others which have pointed out the same thing.

Caseloads of sixty to eighty are not uncommon at the present time, contrasted with the one hundred to one hundred twenty-five of a few years ago. This becomes increasingly possible as the supply of speech pathologists in some states is meeting or exceeding the demands for this service in the states.

During the first week or two of school, the speech pathologists should screen all children who are new to the school district and rescreen those with whom they worked the previous year. It is from this screening that the caseload for the coming year is built. Where more than one pathologist is employed, this screening can be done on a team basis. This makes it possible to schedule a complete school in a short period of time, and this seems to interfere less with getting school underway than to stretch out the screening over several weeks.

One of the most difficult assignments for the speech pathologist is to schedule the actual correction time. Teachers want this service, but they are reluctant to change their own schedules to make it possible for a pathologist to have a reasonable working schedule. It must be remembered that the pathologists may be working with children from two or three different classes at the same time because of their common problem and it is up to the regular class teachers to get together with the pathologist to arrange a mutually satisfactory time for correction. Recognizing that a pathologist may serve several schools, it can be seen that concessions should be made to the pathologist rather than to the regular class teacher.

We are seeing more and more speech pathologists who specialize in an area such as cerebral palsy, mental retardation, and cleft palate. These are usually pathologists who have taken advanced work in one of these specialty areas and a large district should have a number of these highly trained pathologists to work with the more severely involved organic problems of children.

There is considerable controversy over the role of the speech pathologist in language development of school children. Certainly speech pathologists have some skills to contribute to the language development of children, but it would appear that the primary responsibility for language development lies with the regular classroom teacher with consultation from the speech pathologist or anyone else who has expertise to contribute. Certainly speech pathologists may be employed for the specific purpose of the improvement of language, but then they should not be called speech pathologists. Instead they should be identified as language development specialists.

For many years speech pathologists were minimally trained to work with children who were hard of hearing. This, however, is also becoming passé as more public school programs for the hard of hearing are being initiated. What is happening is a greater role differentiation on the part of specialists. Many of the roles were previously assumed by one specialist or another because of the shortage of specifically trained staff.

MENTALLY RETARDED

Schools in general have assumed responsibility for two of the three groups of the mentally retarded, these being educable mentally retarded and trainable mentally retarded. Although there are still many school districts which do not have programs for the trainable, there are still others who are receiving pressure from their communities to provide programs for the most severely retarded and are being required to do so because of recently enacted legislation. The philosophical arguments over the school's role for the trainable and more severely retarded generally hinge on the responsibility of the various agencies of the state governments; that is, education and mental health. Only one state at this point has the trainable program under the jurisdiction of mental health, all others have them under the jurisdiction of the department of education. Missouri has a unique arrangement in that programs for the trainable mentally retarded are operated directly by the state, except in St. Louis County where they are operated by the Special School District.

The current practice of returning institutionalized mentally retarded persons to the community is forcing the schools to replan their programs for the mentally retarded in cooperation with state departments of mental health (or other agencies having responsibility for institutions).

Table I outlines an educational ladder for the mentally retarded, showing the traditional arrangement of classes for the educable and trainable. The breakdown for education is as follows: primary, intermediate, junior high school and senior high school. The ladder for trainable is as follows: primary, intermediate, adolescent I and adolescent II. The children in the educable curriculum ladder are usually children with IQ's between 50 and 75, and in the trainable ladder 25 to 50. There are some factors influencing this educational ladder at the present time. They are as follows:

TABLE I

TYPICAL SCHOOL LADDER FOR THE MENTALLY RETARDED

Educable IQ's 50-75		Trainable IQ's 25-49	
SENIOR HIGH SCHOOL Ages 16+ Vocational		ADOLESCENT II Ages 16+ Work training	
JUNIOR HIGH SCHOOL Ages 12-15 Academic Prevocational		ADOLESCENT I Ages 12-15 Socialization Prework experience	
ELEMENTARY SCHOOL—Intermediate Ages 9-11 Academic		INTERMEDIATE Ages 9-11 Self-care Socialization	
ELEMENTARY SCHOOL—Primary Ages 6-8 Readiness and Academic		PRIMARY Ages 6-8 Self-care	

1. Court decisions have clearly pointed to the fact that children who are functioning as educable retarded because of cultural deprivation most likely will no longer be placed in special classes, if not by school district and administrative policy decision, then by court order (Table I). There are a number of cases involving minority groups to show the direction in which this program is going. These children are generally of the higher levels of the educable classification, and although special classes *can* give them the remedial type of program they need, all too often they do not. Some programs give remedial help, but they stigmatize the children in the process. The fact seems to be that these children are going to be placed in regular classes and it

behooves school administrators to begin to prepare for this movement. There seems to be no question that school districts which
continue to place culturally deprived children who are functioning as retarded in special classes for the mentally retarded are
in for difficult times.

2. Another factor which is changing the complexion of the
structure of special classes for the mentally retarded is the fact
that an examination of the characteristics of the children on the
lower end of the educable range and the upper end of the trainable range clearly show that they are more homogeneous in
their characteristics than the children on the bottom and top
ends of each of these separate categories. This is illustrated
when one attempts to move a lower-level educable child from
an elementary to a junior high school and finds that he cannot
remember his locker combination, cannot remember his schedule
of classes, has none of the basic skills to be integrated into a
single program, and in general "sticks out like a sore thumb" and
in so doing stigmatizes the whole class. This can be overcome
by following the program configuration in Table II. This table
shows that the junior high-age children from both the trainable
and educable level (upper end of trainable and lower end of
educable) can be put together to form a middle group. Sometimes this group is called moderately dependent educable. This
group, along with the trainable, can be easily housed in separate
facilities; in fact, it is easier to provide an adequate school
program for them in a separate facility than in a program in
which they would be integrated into a regular school. Thus,
the higher-level residual in the junior and senior high school are
those youngsters who would be aimed at competitive employment and would become relatively independent upon completion
of their schooling. The middle group will most likely be placed
in sheltered employment and will always require some supervision of their activities. The lowest group is usually not
employable except in the most sheltered environments.

Generally, one would expect 2 percent of the school population to fall into the classification of educable mentally retarded
and two tenths of 1 percent to be classified as trainable, with a

TABLE II

PROPOSED SCHOOL LADDER FOR THE MENTALLY RETARDED

IQ 75	65±	60±	40±	25	IQ 25>
Educable IQ's 65–75±		Moderately Dependent IQ's 40–65±	Trainable IQ's 25–40±	Severe IQ's 25>	
SENIOR HIGH SCHOOL Ages 16+ Vocational Preparation		ADOLESCENT II Ages 16+ Work Training	ADOLESCENT II Ages 16+ Work Training		Socialization
JUNIOR HIGH SCHOOL Ages 12–15 Academic plus Vocational Exploration		ADOLESCENT I Ages 12–15 Academic Prework Training	ADOLESCENT I Ages 12–15 Socialization Prework Exploration		Language
ELEMENTARY SCHOOL Intermediate Ages 9–12 Academic		INTERMEDIATE Ages 9–11 Academic	INTERMEDIATE Ages 9–11 Skills for Protection		
ELEMENTARY SCHOOL Primary Ages 6–8 Diagnostic Placement Readiness		PRIMARY Ages 6–8 Socialization Readiness	PRIMARY Ages 6–8 Socialization Self Care		Self Care
PRESCHOOL Ages 0–5 Language Acquisition		PRESCHOOL Ages 0–5 Language Socialization Self Care	PRESCHOOL Ages 0–5 Language Self Care		

 Represents the level of mental retardation in which "mainstreaming" will most likely be successful. It is largely made up of children who are loosely defined as being mentally retarded from "unknown causes".

still smaller number classified as severely mentally retarded. To illustrate the point of the impact of cultural deprivation the author cites the instance of two communities in St. Louis County. One had an average income of $27,000 and the schools were spending about $1,000 per child on regular class programs and taxing themselves at the rate of $2.68 per thousand of assessed evaluation. Every mentally retarded child in that community was known and they numbered less than one half of 1 percent. Almost all of them were in the range below 65 IQ and most had been placed in private facilities. The other community had an average income of approximately $4,000, was spending about $350 per child for regular education as opposed to a $550 county average, but were taxing themselves at the rate of $4.00 per $1,000. Using the same testing criteria as used in the first community, 33 percent of the school population would have qualified as being educable mentally retarded. The problem there was not one of mental retardation primarily, but rather one of upgrading the total school system. Fortunately, Title I of the Elementary and Secondary Education Act has made significant strides in that school system. There are too many communities, however, which are still attempting to place all of these children in special classes for the retarded. As a result the parents are getting up in arms, going to court, and winning the cases. It is this group of children for whom "mainstreaming" is most appropriate.

An examination of the educational ladder on page 76 shows that in the educable group, the primary level has the major emphasis on diagnostic and readiness activities, the intermediate level on academic skills, the junior high on continuation of academic skills plus the introduction of vocational skills, and the senior high the major emphasis is on vocational preparation. The trainable group, however, shows that the major emphasis at the primary level is on self-care and socialization; the intermediate level emphasis is on socialization and learning skills for their own protection. At the adolescent I and adolescent II level there is a continuation of these skills plus the introduction of skills leading to limited economic usefulness. The school program for the severely impaired largely revolves around self-care, socialization skills and the acquisition of language.

It is sometimes difficult to convince a parent to place a child in a special class at age six and, although it has been done many times, the author has what is considered to be a more professionally defensible plan. This is to consider the primary classes for the educable as passé. Instead, we should develop primary classes for a series of handicapped children and operate them as diagnostic classes. This will sort out the children with learning disabilities, cultural deprivation, and other problems including mental retardation. Children would stay in such a developmental program for a maximum of three years (as a general rule). If they developed the necessary skills, they would move on into regular classes or other specialized facilities. The residual would be the truly mentally retarded.

Another controversial area is that of the school's role in job placement. Certainly with the advent of earmarked money under the Vocational Education Act amendments of 1968, the school must assume an increasing role in work-study and, the author believes, in job placement. Many states today are operating in cooperation with the Vocational Rehabilitation Administration with VRA staff doing the job placement and supervision and the schools providing the academic or skill training within the school setting. The one hazard of this arrangement is that there may not be adequate feedback from the job to the teacher so that the child can be more adequately trained to take his place in the job market. It would appear that the marriage of VRA and the schools has been a marriage of convenience so that VRA can qualify for additional funds.

Generally, children are placed in work settings in the eleventh and twelfth years of their school experience. During the eleventh year they are placed in the school, i.e. cafeteria or custodial, and in the twelfth year in the community.

Frequently the schools are asked to take on the role of operating a sheltered workshop. The author does not feel that this is a proper role for the school to assume and that a sheltered workshop should be operated by either a private or state agency other than the schools. The rationale for this opinion is that the school is a "moving through" process, and that the possibility of getting into long-range, perhaps lifetime operations with an individual (not affiliated with further or advanced training) is outside the province of the school.

The author has frequently been asked at what level a school district should start a program for the retarded, particularly the educable retarded. The advice is invariably to start at the earliest legal level possible, and yet this advice is rarely taken because the pressures on the superintendent and the board of education are to start programs at the later elementary and perhaps junior high level. All too often, in the early elementary grades a child is given a social promotion and it is not until he is sitting in the third grade for perhaps the second time that it occurs to someone that this child is going nowhere in the regular class and that he needs some specialized help. Waiting until this time for a complete diagnosis and possible placement in a special class is unforgiveable, because the child's attitudes towards school and life are so warped by this time that the special class teacher can do little to assist him, and yet will be held responsible for his academic achievement as well as his behavior pattern in the school. This obviously is not fair to either the child or the teacher. With the diagnostic skills that professionals should have today, there is no rationale for keeping a child in a setting which is obviously unfavorable to his development. Certainly, the role of the administrator is to press for the development of facilities for children with these problems.

EMOTIONALLY DISTURBED

Although Eli Bower[1] in his book, *Early Identification of the Emotionally Disturbed Children in School* describes five levels of severity which can be taken into consideration when planning for the treatment and education of emotionally disturbed children, for educational purposes three levels are usually sufficient. For educational planning the three levels can best be characterized by the degree of severity and the required school placement and auxiliary services necessary to make it possible for a given child to function. The most severe, of course, are those children who cannot, even with adequate supportive services, function in a public school setting. These are the children who would require a closed or residential setting where the therapy given is more important, or takes precedence over the educational program even though the educational program would be considered a part of the therapy process. Even though such children are not generally educated in the schools it is important for special educators and others to know that facilities for such children do exist because it is frequently necessary to refer children to a more sheltered setting than is available in the school.

The two disturbance levels with which schools are most concerned are what might be considered mild and moderate. Most of the children who would be classified as having emotional disturbance would fall in the mild group. By and large, these children can attend regular classes assuming that they have the support of adequate counseling, social work help, psychological counseling, and, where necessary, psychiatric treatment. Unfortunately, many children who require such services do not receive them until their problems become rather severe. This is truly a case where "an ounce of prevention is worth a pound of cure." The major emphasis seems to be placed by most schools on children who have more severe problems falling somewhere between the mild group and those requiring more intensive care in a residential facility. The children who tend to get referred for this service are those who are aggressive or acting-out types of children and who are disruptive of the regular classes. Unfortunately, many of the children who are withdrawn do not get referred as readily when, in fact, they may be in more serious difficulty with their emotional problems than those children who are able to relieve their aggression in socially unacceptable ways.

Many of the children who are emotionally disturbed will be referred to the diagnostic staff as being mentally retarded. The reason for this is that their lack of achievement in the regular class makes unsophisticated regular class teachers feel that they have limited capacity for learning, when in fact, the problem is an emotional disturbance which keeps them from focusing on the tasks given them.

One of the prerequisites of a successful program for emotionally disturbed children is that the pupil-teacher ratio be kept relatively low. Depending upon the severity of the disturbances the children exhibit, from six to ten would be considered a load. This ratio could be increased if sufficient aide service is available, as it should be. The basic principle of these classes is to remove the child from the environment which helped to create his emotional disturbance (or at least aided and abetted the creation). The child is placed in a relatively sheltered environment and moved from the sheltered environment to a more complex environment as his emotional skills are improved. This means, of course, that spade work must be done with regular class teachers to accept children who have been placed in classes for the emotionally disturbed as these children are ready to move out. Many regular class teachers are reluctant to accept such children and may even negatively influence such placements because the diagnostic staff is reluctant to place a child knowing that it will be difficult to have him return to the regular class. Such a return has actually become a negotiable item in one of the states which uses master teacher contracts.

There has been some controversy over what philosophy would prevail in classroom management in special classes for the emotionally disturbed. The philosophy varies from one of being extremely permissive to one of being very structured. From a pragmatic point of view, it seems that the structured environment is conducive to better academic achievement and maintenance of behavior patterns than one which is completely permissive. If, however, a child is not able to tolerate the structure on a given day or period, there should be a quiet place where children can feel free to go as they learn the limits of their toleration for the stimulation of classroom activities. An excellent review of the research in this area was made by Frank Hewitt and appears in the *Handbook of Research on Teaching,* published in 1973.[2] Hewitt reviews the various approaches to dealing with emotionally disturbed children and the pertinent research for each approach.

Certainly, any program where there would be special class placement or regular class placement is dependent upon the availability of a number of auxiliary services including the availability of social workers, psychologists, and psychiatrists. Such services are usually considered a legitimate part of the costs of operating such programs.

As was mentioned earlier, at least three levels of programs are essential if emotionally disturbed children are to be served. A school district cannot truly be said to have a complete program if it does not have provisions for children to be placed in regular classes with supplementary services, in special classes which may serve as resource rooms for the children who are on their way to recovery, and in addition, have available by referral a sheltered environment which is most likely residential in nature. In planning a program for the emotionally disturbed these three levels should be built into the plan.

DEAF

One of the major problems in working with the deaf is the fact that there is a schism in this country over which approach to use in teaching them; that is, the oral or manual method. The oral method being the use of speech and speech reading completely without signs and the manual method being either the use of signs or finger spelling. For many years the day schools, which would include all public schools, have concentrated on the oral approach with the basic philosophy that these children will have to live in a hearing world and thus should receive their instruction in, and become proficient in, speech and speech reading (lipreading). State schools, on the other hand, traditionally used the manual approach. These schools still use the manual approach for many children who have not developed acceptable speech. However, in most state schools it is possible at this point to have instruction in either the manual or oral method. There has been a significant change in programs in both the day schools and the state schools in the last ten years, much of it triggered by a study conducted by a committee appointed by Anthony Celebreeze, then Secretary of Health, Education, and Welfare.[3] The report of that committee, presented to the Secretary in 1964, has made major changes in the education of the deaf in many places. It should be pointed out that the state schools for the deaf were the first to change, many of them having added oral programs long before the report was made. It is only in recent years that the day schools have even begun to consider adding the teaching of manual communication at some point in a child's school program. The author has always considered the teaching of manual communication analagous to the teaching of a foreign language in the normal school program. Actually, the finger spelling and basic signs can be taught in a relatively short period of time. The author's reason for insisting that all deaf individuals be able to communicate manually is that it is incongrous to see deaf individuals who cannot communicate with each other orally because their speech is not adequate to be lip-read by another deaf person.

An approach which does not appear to have received widespread attention in this country is that of simultaneous teaching of both finger spelling and lipreading. This work has been pioneered through the Institute of Defectology in the U.S.S.R. and has been reported by a number of investigators who have spent time at the Institutes; the most recent being the report of the delegation of distinguished special educators from the United States who spent three weeks in the U.S.S.R. in late fall of 1972. They report that when very young deaf children are taught by the dual communication method that by the age of seven or eight the finger spelling drops off and the children are almost completely oral.[*]

In line with the concept of "mainstreaming," more and more deaf children are being integrated into regular classes; however, the degree of integration depends upon the language facility of the children and their ability to handle the academic work

---

[*] A delegation sponsored by the Council for Exceptional Children, the Bureau for the Education of the Handicapped, U.S. Office of Education, and the Johnson Foundation, Racine, Wisconsin. The Report was made to Midwest Special Educators on April 12, 1973. Written reports on the visitation are available through the Council for Exceptional Children.

in the regular class. The integration may be for very brief periods in the day or may be relatively extensive. As the children are integrated into the special class, the teacher plays two roles. The first role is the teaching of all things not covered in the regular class including lipreading and speech production. Of course, emphasis is placed on the utilization of residual hearing in these efforts. Secondly, the special class teacher serves as a resource to the regular class teacher. Many regular class teachers are reluctant to accept deaf children into their classes because they feel they will be at a disadvantage in teaching them. However, if they know that someone is behind them to assist when necessary they will be more inclined to accept deaf children in their classes.

Where deaf children are completely integrated into regular class programs (this would be more likely to happen at a junior or senior high school level) they would continue to need supportive services from a specialist in hearing problems. Usually this is provided through an itinerant who would serve many children in a variety of schools. Occasionally resistance to having deaf children integrated into regular classes arises in a community. This may stem from a teacher's reluctance to accept the children or from parents of normal children feeling that the presence of deaf children will usurp the time of the teacher which should be given to their children. There is, however, little evidence to support such contentions. It is extremely important to prepare the class for the acceptance of a deaf child and to prepare the parents of both deaf and normal children for such integration. Any precipitate decision to move from a segregated to an integrated program without adequate preparation for both groups can lead to a series of problems for the school.

The special classes, whether they be relatively self-contained or resource rooms, must be kept quite small. Most states have regulations on the maximum number of children who can be placed in such programs, but generally the numbers would run from four to eight, depending upon the severity of the problems evidenced by the children so placed and the degree to which the children were integrated into regular classes. In smaller communities, a major problem is the age spread of the children

available to make up the classes. In such instances, it is imperative that cooperative arrangements be made so that the catchment area is large enough to make it possible to have classes
that have relatively homogeneous age grouping.

HARD OF HEARING

It goes almost without saying that most hard-of-hearing
children will be found in regular classrooms. This, of course,
is because the hearing losses can be extremely minimal, with
the children needing little or no service. This can range from
the very minor hearing losses which do not usually affect the
academic life of a child to the more severe losses which approach
the category of deafness. The necessary special arrangements
for such children can usually be accomplished with a minimum
of effort, with a major problem being teachers' awareness and
acceptance of the hearing problems. Frequently the only necessary arrangement is that of seating a child in an appropriate place
in a classroom. Most teachers, when asked where they would
seat a hearing-handicapped child in a classroom, would place
him in the front row. This might be appropriate if all the
teacher does is lecture; however, if there is any class interaction
it would be an inappropriate seating arrangement. Rather, the
child should be placed about halfway down a row which is
closest to the windows of the room so that the light is on his
back and on the faces of the individuals in the class. When a
class discussion is being carried on it is possible to develop a
system for identifying who is speaking so that the child with
the hearing handicap can know where to focus his attention.
This is especially important if the child is using a combination
of amplification and lipreading to communicate orally.

Even when hard-of-hearing children are completely integrated
into regular classes many of them will need some supplementary
help from either a speech correctionist or an itinerant hearing
therapist. These professionals can monitor the quality of the
children's speech and assist the regular class teacher on any
problems they might be having in the integrating process.

The more severely hearing handicapped will need more

specialized services. They will need training in the use of hearing aids, both individual and group. The group aids will be utilized when greater amplification is needed for the academic teaching and for their speech training. If the child spends a good portion of the day in a resource room or is in a segregated unit it will be necessary for the teacher not only to be concerned with his speech and language development, but also with his academic attainment. This poses a major problem because of the time utilized in the former to the detriment of the latter. It is because of this dual instructional load that most of our deaf children leave school with an academic retardation. For this reason, it is absolutely essential that children with hearing problems be identified early and be given training in language acquisition and utilization prior to school entrance. In fact, one of the major thrusts leading to the changing of special education laws to include children from zero to twenty-five is the necessity of preschool programs for many of the handicapped so that they may fully participate in school programs.

Most hard-of-hearing children can be integrated into regular classes for a large portion of the school day, with the remainder of the time being spent in a resource room. Here again, the resource teacher also provides support for the regular class teachers. It takes a good deal of coordination between the two groups of professionals to make integration work. If we truly believe in integration (or mainstreaming) for handicapped children, we must have this type of cooperation between the professionals involved.

BLIND

Before any school district can consider that it has a complete program for the blind it must have four levels of programs available. This of course, presupposes a large enough catchment area to include sufficient children to make the programs practically feasible. The four levels are: (1) a state school for the blind, (2) self-contained classrooms, (3) resource rooms, and (4) itinerant services.

A state school for the blind is available in all parts of the

United States, and it is necessary for a number of reasons. First of all, there may be no public school facilities and it might well be the only service available. Even though there may be public school facilities available, it is sometimes necessary to send some children to the state school to remove a child from a home or community situation. Many blind children are greatly over-protected by their parents, and in some instances, the only method of breaking the chain of dependency is to remove the child from the home. Some children have developed such severe emotional problems revolving around their blindness that they cannot be handled adequately in a public school setting.

A self-contained unit in the public schools is only rarely called for, and it frequently can be combined with a resource room. However, some children may need a self-contained setting, par-ticularly if they are seriously academically retarded or have extreme mobility problems. Such classes are, of course, taught by specially trained teachers of the blind.

Most children can participate in a public school setting by being enrolled in a resource room; that is, they are integrated for some portion of the school day in a regular class and return to the resource room for specialized training. Initially the resource room teacher serves as the primary instructional person, giving the children training in the reading and production of braille and other specialized items. As the children develop their skills, they are integrated into regular classes for longer periods of time. As this happens, the resource teacher serves as a support person for the regular class teacher. The support would take a variety of forms, such as assisting the regular class teachers in eliminating their fear of working with blind children. This is necessary because many individuals are extremely frightened of dealing with the blind, feeling that such persons are apt to hurt them-selves, get lost, or some other catastrophe. The support can take other tacks, however, and the ones that are most practical deal with such items as brailling seatwork which the children might have to do in a regular class, brailling tests which will be administered to the class, and the provision of equivalent taped or brailled material or books which the children will be reading in regular classes. The support services of this nature frequently require outside assistance, largely through volunteer help.

It is surprising how completely blind children can be integrated into regular classes. For example, the author has observed blind children who were integrated into first grade running relay races with the normal children, roller skating, playing on the jungle gyms and, although he knew the handicapped children, he found it difficult in many instances to detect which of the children were blind. He even observed blind children riding bicycles. We are too prone to prevent blind children from participating in many activities in which they could and should be allowed to determine for themselves what they can and cannot do. The stereotype of a handicap is no more firmly ingrained in the public mind than in the area of the blind.

A plan for providing itinerant support services is excellent for those who have developed their academic skills and their mobility skills. Usually such a plan is most successful at the secondary school level. Here again, there is a great need for volunteers to braille materials and to record on tape books and exercises.

Public schools are eligible for assistance from the American Printing House for the Blind through their state schools for the blind. Money is allocated to the state for every blind child in school and these monies are disbursed through the state schools. Another resource available to public schools is the "talking books" program of the Library of Congress, available through regional libraries for the blind. Some districts have also established exchange programs for locally produced items of both braille and tape recordings.

A major consideration in providing public school programs for the blind is the organization necessary to have brailled or taped materials in a classroom exactly when needed. The author has frequently stated that it takes up to six volunteers in the community to support any one child in a completely integrated setting. The Library of Congress does have a certification program for those who wish to learn how to write braille, and most schools will have to rely on people who have had this kind of training. If trained people are not available, the director of special education, or the teacher for the blind, or whoever else is responsible for the program should organize a community training program to develop a cadre of volunteers who are willing to take the training and produce materials at an acceptable level. Another group of volunteers can be utilized in the production of tapes. It is one thing to record a novel in acceptable fashion and quite another to record a book on physics. All of the items in the physics book which depend upon sight have to be translated to another sense. The author has found that retired professionals frequently are an excellent source of personnel in producing such materials.

A necessary part of the training of any school child is what is known as "orientation and mobility." This is the skill necessary to move around comfortably and safely in a given locality with the aid of a long cane. Although the national press gives much attention to the use of leader dogs, it is unusual to find such a service being used by school children. Even very young school children can learn to move around the school with ease and safety if they are adequately trained to be mobile. Much of the time in the early weeks of the school year could well be devoted to such training. Specialists are available to provide this orientation and mobility training. They are being educated in a number of institutions of higher education in the United States and in foreign countries; however, the greatest impetus for this training has come from Western Michigan University, Kalamazoo. It is frequently possible to develop cooperative relationships with other agencies for the joint use of the services of such professionals.

There has been considerable experimental work done on electronic devices to assist the blind. One of these is the use of ultrasonic glasses, which is a sort of "radar system" which provides auditory signals to the individual when he approaches obstacles. Another device for improving mobility is the laser cane. These are promising developments which may revolutionize the mobility of blind people if they are able to be trained in their use. Still another item is a device which allows blind individuals to read standard printed material. This device, called the *Optacon,* scans individual letters and translates them into tactual signals. As these devices become more available, it is essential that the schools assist their blind students to receive training in their use, or at the very least, to cooperate with other agencies who are providing such training. No stone should be left unturned to assist these people to lead as normal a life as possible.

PARTIALLY SIGHTED

As with the hard of hearing there are relatively large numbers of partially sighted children, but only the more severely involved need special facilities. Many need only some attention to the lighting in a classroom and to their seating position. It was not many years ago that the major problem for the partially sighted was poor lighting in the classroom; however, the quality of classroom lighting has improved so much that the general lighting in newly constructed buildings is equivalent to that which was standard in classrooms for the partially sighted fifteen or twenty years ago.

For those who do need special help, training in the use of their residual vision and in conserving the vision they have must be provided. For those with a prognosis of eventual blindness, some early training in braille may be started.

The books and other printed materials used in instruction are of the large type variety. Such books are extremely expensive, being five to six times the cost of a standard book. One of the largest publishers of such books is Stanwix House. Recently the federal government has supported the development of large type materials in other forms. The Michigan School for the Blind, for example, has experimented with new processes and formats.

It is usually necessary to have special types of paper available for the partially sighted to use. This is sometimes called "eye-saver" paper because it is nonglare and contributes to the sight conservation program.

Usually two types of special instructional arrangements are adequate to meet the needs of most partially sighted children.

These would be resource rooms, where the children would receive the special training mentioned above and any tutoring in the academic subjects they were taking in regular classes. The second type would be an itinerant service where the children are integrated into the regular classes for 100 percent of the time. Here the specially trained teacher would spend time interpreting to the regular class teacher the needs of the partially sighted children and in providing materials and/or some specialized tutoring.

ORTHOPEDICALLY HANDICAPPED

At times the term *crippled and other health impaired* is used instead of orthopedically handicapped; however, the latter term seems to be more definitive than the former. The standard definition of orthopedic handicap is a defect of the bone, muscle, or joint. Under this rubric, one can include children with heart problems, arthritis, cerebral palsy, muscular dystrophy, and any other physical condition which affects a child's ability to utilize his body normally.

There was a time when roughly one-third of the classes for orthopedically handicapped were those who had had polio, one-third had cerebral palsy, and one-third had miscellaneous defects. Fortunately, that situation had changed with the advent of the antipolio vaccines. Today the mix is approximately one-half cerebral palsied and the other half miscellaneous defects. It should seem obvious that this group of children known as orthopedically handicapped is not a homogeneous group, rather it is an extremely heterogeneous group with wide variations in intellectual and physical abilities (or disabilities). This makes programming for them an essentially individual matter. Nevertheless, classes for them are usually divided into primary, intermediate, junior and senior high school levels. In order to obtain the services of a physical or occupational therapist, it is almost essential that three classes be housed in the same building so that the school district can get maximum utilization of the services of the ancillary services. It must be anticipated that the special class placement is a long-range plan for some children. One might anticipate this for children with conditions such as muscular dystrophy or severe cerebral palsy. Other children, however, need only a short-term placement. This might be true of children such as one who had a leg amputated in a boating accident. He was a high school student and as soon as he was released from the hospital he was placed in a special class where he was kept up in his academic work, but in addition, through the work of the therapists, his stump was prepared for the acceptance of a prosthetic device. As soon as the device was made, it was fitted and he was taught how to use it properly. In a matter of months he began to play baseball and shortly after he returned to his regular high school class.

There is nothing really very magic about a special class for orthopedically handicapped children, although it seems that way when one observes such a class in operation. Rather, it is an intense concern for the individual needs of the children, both from a physical and instructional point of view. The subject matter of instruction covers the usual items found in elementary and secondary school curricula, if the children have the intellectual capability of profiting from such instruction. For those children who do not have this intellectual capacity, it is possible to develop cooperative programs with classes dealing with intellectual deficit. For example, a child might be placed in a classroom for trainable mentally retarded for his "academic" instruction, but he may be in a building where supportive services such as physical and occupational therapy are available to him. Some state regulations specify that to be eligible for a class for the orthopedically handicapped the children must have "normal" intelligence. With careful planning of the placement of classes, it is possible to make the ancillary services available to all of those children who can profit from them. Much of the special consideration for the orthopedically handicapped was dealt with in the section on physical facilities because it is the adaptation of the physical space that the child uses that makes a difference as to whether or not he can survive in the school.

More and more emphasis is being placed on the learning problems of children in classes for the orthopedically handicapped because they are coming more and more from backgrounds stemming from neurologic problems. A neurologic problem does not necessarily confine itself to the physical aspects of an individual, but more often than not, there is generalized central nervous system damage which will also affect his learning abilities. It can be seen that it is important for a teacher working in this area to be conversant, not only with the physical manipulations which are necessary, but with the techniques of working with the mentally retarded and learning disabled. It is for this reason that some states are beginning to move toward including specific training in learning disabilities for the training of teachers of all handicapped children.

In the last ten years there has been increasing concern over the provision of services for the very seriously disabled. For example, in 1956 the author evaluated a school program in Michigan where all of the children were ambulatory, that is, no one was in a wheel chair and all of those who did use crutches were able to move around freely. In questioning the educational and medical leaders in the community, it was revealed that they felt that the more severely handicapped children could not go to school. This is contrasted with the philosophy espoused by Henry Viscardi, Director of the Human Resources, Inc., of Albertson, New York. He feels that all children, no matter how seriously impaired, have a right to attend school, and he does indeed have extremely handicapped children in his school program, some attending school in litters with such things as library shelves nearly at floor level so that the children can select their own books. With the advent of modern, one-story school buildings, many children who were previously attending classes for the orthopedically handicapped because they could not manage the steps in the regular school are now happily enrolled in regular classes or "mainstreamed" as they should be.

With the elimination or amelioration of many of the medically oriented problems, it has been said that the field of working with the orthopedically handicapped is a dying field, but this is truly an area where education continues to "pick up the pieces." If, as it appears, we are moving into a period of realistic genetic counseling and therapeutic abortions, many of the types of children we currently see in classes for the orthopedically handicapped will have either disappeared or have been drastically reduced.

Parent counseling is probably more essential in working with the orthopedically handicapped than any other area. This is not only at intake time, but throughout the child's school life. Both parents and children develop unrealistic aspiration levels and many of the children develop emotional problems relating to their physical handicap. Counseling of both parents and children is especially important when children have degenerative diseases, such as muscular dystrophy or when the condition is brought on by trauma. More people, including parents, would seem to approach Samuel Laycock's level one of acceptance with the severely involved orthopedically handicapped than in any other area of handicap. It is very difficult to feel as close to a severely involved child if he has a gross physical handicap than if he has a normal physical appearance. A part of the school training program for such children should be designed to help them know how other people view them and how they should react to those who obviously react negatively. With such training they may be able to maintain the ego strength necessary to continue to survive. Without special assistance they will not "make it" as a human being.

LEARNING DISABLED

The term "learning disabilities" is a relatively new term in educational jargon. Interest in the group of children described as having learning disabilities came from both educators and physicians concurrently. Some of the early research done by educators such as Kirk, then at the University of Illinois; Myklebust, then at Northwestern University; Kephart, then at the University of Indiana; Harring, then at the University of Kansas Medical Center, set the stage for educators interested in these children. Much of the interest was triggered by a concern for the lack of language development or deviant language and motor development in children. At about the same time, some physicians were becoming concerned over a group of children they called *hyperkinetic.* The result of these diverse interests was the fact that many people were describing the same kinds of children with different names. In fact, Robert Hall, who was with the U.S. Office of Education in the capacity of Consultant on crippled and other health impaired, wrote and talked about "The Child with Too Many Names." Some of the names used are: hyperkinetic, neurologically impaired, perceptually handicapped, brain injured, and learning disabled. The interest has gradually changed from those children with more severe problems to those who do not necessarily have positive neurological involvement, or are not mentally retarded or emotionally disturbed. The best way to describe the term "learning disability" is that it is a generic term rather than a specific term. In other words, a child who is mentally retarded may have a learning disability and a child who is gifted may also have a learning disability. In fact, it may be sometimes difficult to tell which came first, the learning disability or the other diagnoses of emotional disturbance, or mental retardation.

During the 1964-67 period, the position of the Special Educators in the U.S. Office of Education (at least during the time the author was there) was that we were developing a series of cults around this new terminology based on the key individuals who were promoting different kinds of treatment programs. We took it as a major goal to try to keep lines of communication open between the various subgroups so that identifiable training programs could be determined for funding purposes. At that time, there was no agreed upon criteria for what constituted an adequate training program (and to this day there is no *clear-cut* agreement on this).

Because of increasing national interest in the problem, various units in the Department of Health, Education, and Welfare (including the U.S. Office of Education and the National Institute of Child Health and Development) cooperated with the National Society for Crippled Children and Adults to sponsor three task forces to make recommendations in the area. The charge for Task Force One was to come up with a definition which would be acceptable. Unfortunately, this Task Force was largely medically oriented and, as a result, the definition made the major assumption that for a child to be considered as having a learning disability there must be some neurological signs of impairment. Task Force Two dealt with the treatment which would be necessary, both educationally and medically. Because of the educators not accepting the definition of Task Force One, they took it upon themselves to expand the definition to include children who do not show positive neurological damage. Task Force Three dealt with the problem of needed research, both in education and medicine. (The reports of all three of these task forces are available from the U.S. Government Printing Office.)

The number of students considered to have learning disabilities has never been adequately determined. The Bureau for Education of the Handicapped in the U.S. Office of Education is still using a figure of 1 to 2 percent for its planning purposes. However, estimates run as high as 20 to 25 percent. These estimates can be justified only as one includes all children who are not learning in regular classrooms by the usual methods of instruction.

It would seem that the only position one can take, considering the definition which has been adopted by the Council of Exceptional Children—Division of Children with Learning Disabilities, and the Association for Children with Learning Disabilities, and which seems to be accepted by educators nationally, is to consider the work with children having learning disabling conditions as a teaching technique based on an understanding of the various disabilities, the ability to diagnose these disabilities and, finally, to prescribe a treatment program carrying out the appropriate remedial program.

The end result of such a position will be a necessity for both special educators and general educators to be trained in the area of learning disabilities. In most teacher-training programs for special education, this is already being woven into the training programs for all teachers of handicapped children.

With the percentage of children estimated to have learning disabilities, it would appear that all teachers, especially elementary teachers, must have skills in working with these children. This can either be built into the existing theory and methods courses or added to current requirements, although the former would appear to be preferable. (This assuming the staff can be retrained to be knowledgeable about learning disabilities and be given some insight into how this can be included in the general information now being taught in college classes.) Certainly consideration must be given to the desirability of spelling out such a training requirement in certification regulations.

The role of special education staff who are more intensively trained would be to work with the more severely disabled in teaching situations outside of the regular classrooms. In addition, such staff could and should serve as resource personnel to regular class teachers who are untrained or minimally trained in working with children having learning disabilities.

In summary, it appears that after six or seven years of "milling around" between people who consider themselves specialists in the area of learning disabilities, general education is becoming alert to the idea that many of these children can and should be in the regular classrooms. They have further concluded that general educators will need some specific training in working with these children. An examination of most training programs will reveal that there is nothing very magical about what is being done. Rather, remediation is a strict application of diagnosis, prescription, and remediation and this should be the aim of all educators who are working with handicapped children in a special class, handicapped children in a regular class or nonhandicapped children in a regular class. Thus, there is a role for both the special educators and the general educators in working with children who may be diagnosed as having learning disabilities. At all costs, we should avoid a jurisdictional fight over this area. Rather, the position should be that regular educators and special educators be required to develop a working relationship which will assume adequate training for each teaching classification. It would appear that with this area we have a great opportunity to begin to draw special education and regular education together so that they are considered as part of the continuum of educational services rather than as discreet programs.

MAINSTREAMING

As more and more handicapped children are being returned to regular classes for all or part of the school day, there is a necessity for school districts to develop support services for these children. This may take the form of itinerant staff who will work with the regular class teacher in selecting appropriate materials and methods for use with the handicapped. It may take the form of resource rooms where the children can go for a part of the school day for specific instruction or tutorial work. Many teachers who work in resource rooms have been trained to work with more than one type of handicap. In smaller areas such an arrangement may be a necessity if this group of handicapped children is going to be served.

Merely placing a child in a regular classroom does not eliminate his problems and if he is placed without help for the teacher he might well be better served if left in a special class.[4] The continuum of special education services should include the use of itinerant and resource room staff as intermediate points along the continuum where the child can be placed if needed. These services act as a bridge between the special class and the regular class and will make it possible for many children to begin or maintain their activities in the mainstream without feeling the full pressure of complete participation in the regular class.

REFERENCES

1. Bower, Eli: *Early Identification of Emotionally Handicapped Children in School.* Springfield, Thomas, 1960, 8-10.
2. Travers, Robert: *Second Handbook of Research on Teaching.* American Educational Research Association, Chicago, Rand McNally, 1973, 657-688.
3. *Education of the Deaf, A Report to the Secretary of Health, Education, and Welfare by His Advisory Committee on the Education of the Deaf.* Department of Health, Education, and Welfare, March 1965, 1-103.
4. Martin, Edwin: Some thoughts on mainstreaming. *Except Child, 41*:3, 150-154, Nov. 1974.

CHAPTER SIX

PUBLIC INFORMATION

O<small>NE</small> <small>MIGHT</small> <small>WELL</small> <small>ASK</small>, If a school district is performing its job satisfactorily, why does it need any formalized public information or public relations program to tell the public about it?[1] Unfortunately, there are many people in the communities of this nation who really care very little about the success or failure of the schools and this, of course, is intensified when it comes to programs for the handicapped which may be considered as an unnecessary frill. A question frequently raised by the uninformed is, Why do you want to educate these children in the first place when they are not going to amount to anything?

Literally, a public information or public relations program is carried on to inform the public. In so doing, the district projects a positive or negative image by the activities that are carried on and the means by which they are reported. Frequently, the process of carrying on the activities may well be as important as the activities themselves.

The major goals of a public information program are summarized as follows:

1. *To report to the constituency which is paying the bills.* No one wants to see his money spent without an accounting of the ways in which it is spent and without some voice in its expenditure.

2. *To enlist public support.* Obviously, schools cannot continue to operate unless they have the support of at least a majority of the people who live in the community. The most obvious form of support is, of course, whether or not the people

are willing to tax themselves to support the program. Too often, the only time school administrators attempt to get the support is at the time of tax levies. The kind of support which is desperately needed in our schools, not only for the handicapped, but for all types of education, is a truly emotionally gripping kind of support which is evidenced by the local tax payers literally demanding good services for the children of the community.

3. Public relations will assist in the recruitment of adequate staff. Good teachers will gravitate to schools where there is good community support and administrator support for the programs in which they are interested. An excellent staff then provides still better programs and the support is enhanced.

4. Another role of public relations is to project a professional climate for the professionals working in the field and to the professional associations to which these people belong. This is obviously tied up with item three above. For example: At one point the author arranged through a coordinator of speech and hearing to send thirty speech therapists to the national convention of the American Speech and Hearing Association. Each section of that convention was "covered" by a staff member who attended. Through discussion, this staff member identified himself as being from that district. The result was an influx of applications from individuals who had masters degrees and full certification from the American Speech and Hearing Association, so that for three openings there were over two hundred applications. This is an example of a public information activity which projected a professional climate which led to better recruiting, which in turn led to increased public support for the program.

Many years ago Samuel Laycock, University of Saskatoon, enunciated the idea of three levels of acceptance of handicapped children. The first was an aversion to handicapped individuals to the point where the individual would go out of his way to avoid speaking, touching, or having anything to do with the handicapped. The second level was an intellectual acceptance of the fact that handicapped individuals do exist and that they need services. The final level was a complete intellectual and emotional acceptance of the handicapped, recognizing that they have the same needs, desires, and aspirations as the non-handicapped. Very few individuals achieve the third level of acceptance. This includes many teachers who work with the handicapped. However, most of our campaigns, such as the community chest or drives for organizations such as Muscular Dystrophy, Cerebral Palsy, and Mental Retardation, etc. are aimed at the middle level of acceptance and quite successfully. To carry on a realistic public information campaign in a given community, one must recognize that the great bulk of the public is at the second level. However, we should be attempting to move at least some individuals to the higher level of acceptance so that they can serve as catalysts for increased understanding.

It is very easy to fall into the trap of carrying on a completely emotional campaign when dealing with the handicapped. To be against programs for the handicapped is akin to being against home, mother, and the flag. We may well do handicapped individuals a disservice by creating too great an emotional appeal. It should be used judiciously, much as the leavening in bread.

The basic principle of public information for a school district is that one person must be responsible for all official public releases for the district. This does not mean to say that many people will not be speaking to PTA's, church groups, service clubs, and the like. However, if more than one person issues "official" statements about program plans, etc., it is very easy for the public to become confused, particularly if the releases are not coordinated. The annual publication of the American Association of School Administrators of 1953 dealt with the general topic of school public relations.[1] This publication has many helpful suggestions to individuals who wish to develop a public relations program.

There are two major ways in which public information programs can be carried on. The first, of course, is the use of mass media, including newspapers, radio, television, and mass mailings. The second is face-to-face reporting to individuals or organizations. These two approaches will be discussed below.

MASS MEDIA

Newspapers

How does one go about developing a relationship with a major metropolitan daily or perhaps the local paper which is the only paper published in the community? The basic principle is to get to know the person who is setting editorial/reportorial policy and then to get to know the person (on a first name basis) who will be doing the actual writing. This is sometimes easier to do in a "small town" paper than a major metropolitan daily, because on the major papers the person covering the school "beat" will frequently be a "cub" reporter and he may not be on the job for more than a few months so that the school district has to do the informing job over and over again. In any case, one should spend the necessary time with the reporter so that this individual becomes fairly familiar with the hopes, aspirations, problems, and successes of the operation of the school. Visitation to classrooms, pointing out problem areas in buildings or programs helps the reporter to have a perspective in his writing which can be achieved in no other way. All too frequently the only time a reporter has contact with a district is at the time of a board meeting or when an irate parent raises an issue with the school board. Then it is too late for the reporter to achieve the perspective which we all want in our writing. This kind of working relationship, however, makes it possible for the person in charge of public information to call a reporter and say that he has a story which he would like to break at a certain time. This gives the reporter ample time to obtain the facts, cross-check them with reliable sources and report back to the public relations man for the ideas which he is attempting to place in the article. This technique is particularly pertinent for feature articles or major articles about the district. Of course, this is making an assumption that the reporter will be doing the actual writing.

Many school districts write their own releases. This is satisfactory; however, any item which a newspaper receives which is obviously "cranked out" in mass is apt to receive scant attention at the editorial level. Throwaway-type newspapers will accept this type of information, but any paper with a reportorial staff will look at it with some suspicion.

Still another item for consideration is that of balancing releases between newspapers in a given community. No editor likes to be consistently "scooped" on either good or bad news. This creates some difficulties in communities which have morning and evening papers. The morning papers usually get the jump on news coming from board meetings. This means that the public relations person must systematically feed information which is significant to the afternoon newspaper.

In writing releases at the district level, one must remember the basic principle of newspaper writing and that is that the first sentence written is most important. By and large, *editorial* work is from the end of the article, working backwards. All of us have seen news articles in which the last paragraphs say about the same as the first paragraphs. This is because articles are padded or shortened depending upon the space which is available (or needed) for the particular article. Checking with the local papers as to their writing policy will save many articles from being "bobtailed" in the editorial process.

It goes without saying that pictures have to be selected with great care and that no picture of a child will be released without written permission from the child's parents. In addition, one should be extremely careful of showing pictures of severely handicapped children. This is necessary because of what was said earlier about the acceptance level of most people in the community.

One other factor seems worthy of mention. Too frequently the amateur writer attempts to put too many ideas into one newspaper article. The basic principle is that any one article addresses itself to one central idea. If this does not adequately cover the topic, then consideration should be given to writing a series of connected articles around a broad topic with the specifics of any one piece remaining simple. One must remember that the average reader of a newspaper skims for what he wishes to read and if all the "eggs are put into one basket" the headline for the articles may be the one which attracts only a certain set of individuals. For example, mental retardation may appeal to one group, cerebral palsy to another, etc. Thus, a single topic submitted with more frequency will produce greater results.

Radio

Although many people think of the radio only as a record playing, news on the hour, or background sound medium, it must be remembered that it is the constant companion of people at home, in their cars, and in many instances in their offices. Thus, the radio is an ideal medium for getting messages out to the public. Some of the principles of how one goes about working with radio stations are almost identical to how one starts working with newspapers. The individuals responsible for programming must be systematically sought out so that a plan of releases can be made.

The currently popularity of "talk back" shows offers a great opportunity for school people to get their message out and to get problems clarified. There is always a hazard, of course, that only malcontents will call in, but the author's experience does not confirm this suspicion. Rather, the reaction has been one of sincere interest and desire for information from a reliable source.

It should be remembered that both radio and television, by FCC regulations, must devote a percentage of time to public interest broadcasts. Unfortunately, a lot of this time is made available at hours which are not popular, but a reasonable amount of advance planning can work announcements and public information shows into the schedule of popular hours. KMOX in St. Louis has a midafternoon public service show in which they regularly start the program with an individual from an agency or the community who very briefly presents a topic of interest and then opens the telephone lines for discussion. This format has been used by hundreds of radio stations around the country.

It is possible, by working with some of the smaller stations, to present a series of programs dealing with programs for the handicapped or other education matters as well. This activity takes advanced planning between the public relations person and the programming personnel of the station.

Television

Practically everything that was said about radio applies to television programming as well. The one caution in television activities is the presenting of children on the program. The same caution concerning releases of pictures is apropo here. The author's experience has been that, whenever possible, children should be presented *along with* their parents. This apparently helps make the transition from a purely intellectual to the emotional approach of acceptance—developing the feeling of "There but for the grace of God. . . ." Many parents are very capable and willing to endure this kind of exposure because they know it will eventually result in better educational programming for their children.

Here again, television producers are reluctant to have very handicapped children appear on the television screen. Frequently it is possible to work out a program with the parents participating so that no questions need be asked about permission or propriety.

Mass Mailing

The technique of mass mailing or mass distribution of a flyer is frequently used to publicize the school districts. However, it is a process which many times is little understood and, as a result, it is too often misused. These pieces are frequently prepared with the idea of presenting the best possible image of the school district, and the result is that the same techniques used by a major manufacturing firm in selling its products or in presenting an annual report is used for the schools. One must analyze such a production in terms of the image which it projects. Some of the salient factors are as follows:

1. High-gloss, half-tone picture brochures present a picture of affluence.
2. The image schools try to project is one of need or at least reporting to the public with a minimum of expense.
3. The appeal must be made to persons of all socioeconomic levels and perhaps shaded toward the lower end of the scale.

4. The message must be analyzed in terms of the language used so that educational jargon is largely eliminated. If not eliminated, it must be explained.
5. The message must be kept simple; that is, a single message to one document.
6. The brochure must be prepared with a judicious use of color in such a way that it is an immediate eye catcher.
7. Pen and ink drawings of handicapped children and the equipment they use are preferred over actual photographs. (One can identify in a broader way with a sketch more easily than with a specific photograph of a specific child who may well be known in the community.)

In keeping with the economy image which should be projected as much as possible, small "throwaway" type brochures should be distributed by individuals whenever possible. Organizing and carrying out the distribution of such a public relations effort is an excellent project for parents of handicapped children and their interested friends. One can rest assured that if a parent of a handicapped child distributes the brochure and has a chance to talk to other individuals about the contents, there is an emotional involvement on the part of the recipient he would not have if such a piece were delivered to him in his mailbox as part of a bulk mailing. It is recognized that all too often the only method available for the distribution of a brochure is through bulk mailing. However, it should also be recognized that this is a less effective means of distributing such literature than by hand delivery.

Many churches, service clubs, professional organizations, and other groups of this nature will allow such mass literature to be distributed through their membership mechanism, or at least made available for interested individuals to pick up.

Face-to-Face Presentations

A well-developed set of slides or films should be available to individuals from the schools who are making presentations to various organizations such as the Lion's Club, Kiwanis, Rotary, Sertoma, etc. Each of these organizations has its own special interest and the slides or films can be sorted in such a way that a special set can be prepared for each group's interest. This does not mean to say that one should not attempt to broaden the perspective of a particular service club; however, realistically the major thrust of the presentation should be toward the special interest of the particular group.

Churches, with their women's and men's organizations are logical groups to enlist in publicizing efforts made on behalf of handicapped children. Frequently they are looking for stimulating programs and the obvious social worth of what is being done for an unfortunate part of the population fits into the general interest of church organizations.

Each chapter of the national parent-teacher association must, by constitution and bylaws, have a committee dealing with education of exceptional children. Arrangements can be made so that at least one of the programs during the school year deals with some aspect of school programs for the handicapped child. It has been the author's experience that too frequently these committees are uninformed about the nature of the task and welcome the assistance from professionals in the field in helping them to carry out their mission.

Naturally, where there are parent organizations which deal with handicapped children, these should be a major source of face-to-face contact on school programs for handicapped children. Groups such as the Association for Retarded Citizens, United Cerebral Palsy Association, Easter Seal Society, Muscular Dystrophy Association, Nephritis Association, and any other group which has a chapter in the local community should be enlisted as a constant support for the school programs. These organizations are essentially parent-oriented and these are the parents who can "put the heat on" legislators and others who are responsible for public policy which deals with handicapped children. More and more often these organizations are speaking with a combined voice on such problems and, thus, it is essential that the school work well with all agencies.

There is a series of other types of face-to-face contacts which, while they do not fall in the formal public relations domain, certainly help create an image of what the school district is doing for handicapped children. In this category are teacher's meetings, either on a district or on a building base. With more and more of the handicapped children being served in regular classes, good information is becoming more essential to these teachers and every school district should devote a portion of its in-service training time to the problems of the handicapped. There is not a school which does not have in it some children who can be classified as handicapped and thus this topic *should* be of interest to all teachers in the building. All too frequently this problem is the interest of no one and, thus, the children get little support from regular class staff. Some portion of building meetings, either curriculum or human engineering meetings, should be devoted to improving the opportunities of handicapped children in regular classes. Of course, the conversation in the teacher's lounge or coffee room can set the climate for services for handicapped children. If one really wants to probe the climate of acceptance for handicapped children who are in a particular school, one needs only to listen to the coffee room conversation. All of us have had experience with either teachers or administrators expressing their frustrations, lack of ability, or general disinterest in working with children who have learning problems. If teachers of the handicapped are located in such a building they certainly should make every effort to participate in coffee room conversation because of the instructional nature of what can be discussed.

Still another face-to-face contact with the public is the ubiquitous telephone. The voice of the district is the central office operator or the building secretary. Most local telephone companies do carry on programs for working with such people and the image they project. This service should be used on a regular basis. If the telephone answerer wishes to improve his or her skills, one of the techniques which works well is to tape record the first half hour's calls in the morning and the last half hour's in the afternoon. An analysis of these tapes usually shows room for improvement.

Certainly office visits cannot be overlooked in establishing the image or climate of interest. Whenever it is possible school personnel should not put themselves in a position of authority by sitting behind a desk when working with parents. Less formal arrangements, with a cup of coffee or some other refreshment, greatly help to ease the mind of the parent. This is a cardinal principle unless one is consciously structuring the situation so that the parent is being intimidated. Generally, however, the school personnel are attempting to work with the parents and not trying to antagonize them, so the simple matter of making the parent at home in the school domain is important. If this cannot be done comfortably, then the school personnel should go to the parents' domain, whether that is the father's place of business, or at home in the kitchen. The important thing to remember is that the school's image is built on face-to-face contacts.

The final suggestion for face-to-face contacts is to have the special education director, or whoever is responsible for special education, serve on as many boards as he can get appointed or elected to during his initial years in his position. There is so much agency support which is necessary that it is important to know what is going on in other agencies. By accepting board appointments or elections one can get to know what is going on inside these organizations. This is exceedingly time consuming, but it will pay dividends if carried on in the following manner. As reappointments come up the director can, if he wishes, suggest that much as he would like to continue in the post, the press for time precludes such participation. However, he can then suggest that another member of his staff, who has much to contribute, might well be appointed to take his place. This creates a network of participating, knowledgeable people in the community. Such people can help to coordinate services across agencies, and certainly they can carry the message of special education programs into every agency in the community. This, it would appear, is the major rationale for any public information activity.

REFERENCES

1. *Public Relations for America's Schools.* 28th Yearbook, American Association of School Administrators, Washington, D.C., 1953, 1-327.

EPILOGUE

T HE WELL KNOWN quotation, "What is past is prologue" was
never more appropriate than in reviewing the evolution of educational programs for handicapped children. The cycle found in
this century, which has seen the educational community go from
paying little attention to the needs of the handicapped to a
highly systemized complex of special services and then to an
increasing emphasis on returning handicapped children to regular
classrooms, brings us almost full circle in educational philosophy.
However, there are, or should be, major differences between
what we find today and what was prevalent fifty or seventy-five
years ago. Even though the current emphasis is on returning
handicapped children to the regular classroom, there is always
the implication that a series of supportive services will be available to help the children, their teachers, and their parents.
Whether this will be true is up to each of us who has a responsibility for influencing the development or modification of programs in the schools. If we allow children to be "mainstreamed"
without the support services which are so essential for such an
effort to succeed, we will be negating all of the educational
advances made on behalf of handicapped children. The result
will probably be that the whole cycle will have to start over
again, but with greater legal restraints, and with these restraints,
fewer opportunities for professional creativity to influence
programs.

The fact that the courts are so heavily involved in school
decisions affecting handicapped children is something that should
be of concern to all of us. It should be telling us that we have
made some professional decisions which are counter to the mores
of today's society. It means that we have not kept in touch
with the parents of handicapped children, or with the best
information available from our professional sources. The chal-

lenge to provide real leadership in this field is there if we dare to accept it.

The author has had the rare privilege of observing the quantity and quality of concern for handicapped children in many parts of the world. Through such activities one derives the distinct impression that one can measure the level of sophistication of civilization in a country by the concern shown for handicapped children. When a nation must be concerned with hunger and illiterate masses of people there is little effort made on behalf of the handicapped. With the resources available in the United States there can be little excuse for any handicapped person going without all of the services which are necessary for that person's complete habilitation. All it takes is the will to do so and, as educational leaders, we are key figures in expressing that will.

The happiest day in the life of the author or any educator would be the one in which it is found that special education for the handicapped is no longer needed because education and medicine have been able to wipe out any handicaps needing special school provisions. Until that day comes, however, there is a tremendous professional satisfaction in seeing to it that all children, whatever their physical, social, emotional, or mental development, have an opportunity to develop to the full measure of their potential. Special education and general education can share equally in this opportunity.

Handicapped people, both children and adults, long ago taught the author that each day of honest effort, made with a realistic goal in mind, can create minor miracles which, when added together, appear to be a major miracle in which we can all share because they, working together, made it happen. If the suggestions found in these pages can help create a few minor miracles for some handicapped children, then the effort will not have been in vain.

ANNOTATIVE BIBLIOGRAPHY

PHILOSOPHY

Burrello, Leonard; Tracy, Michael, and Schultz, Edward: Special education as experimental education. *Except Child,* 40:1, 29-34, Sept. 1973. 1973.

The authors propose a new conceptualization of special education based on the following:

1. Determination of services on the basis of experimentation and evaluation as opposed to unplanned response to large numbers of children with special needs.

2. Delivery of services with alternative educational opportunities as opposed to continued development of a delivery system within a separate administrative organization.

The authors feel that educators must look more to appropriate alternatives for children rather than relying on the traditional special education model.

Erdman, Robert L.: Declaration of general and special rights of the mentally retarded. *Ment Retard,* 7:4, 2, August 1969.

The author lists the basic rights of the retarded. A retarded person, above all, has the right to respect, and this declaration makes that point clear.

Jones, Reginald: Labels and stigma in special education. *Except Child,* 38:7, 553-564, March 1972.

The author calls attention to various labels and stigmas placed on children and how they feel about certain terms. Surveys of various kinds were used in schools to see if certain special education labels implied deficiencies and shortcomings in children. The surveys showed that children generally rejected labels of *culturally disadvantaged* and *culturally deprived* as being descriptive of themselves. The surveys further showed that acceptance of such labels reflected a low school attitude. In many instances the teachers had lower performance expectations of the deprived and disadvantaged children.

In surveying the educable mentally retarded children, it was found that the children associated a stigma with being placed in a special class labeled as being for EMR. Also, teachers had difficulty developing strategies for managing the stigma of the class.

The authors feel that the use of labels and the stigma they foster has long been neglected.

Jones, Reginald L.: Student views of special placement and their own special classes: A clarification. *Except Child,* 41:1, 22-29, Sept. 1974.

The school morale inventory was given to 341 junior high school retarded students and 717 nonretarded students within the same school. The finding revealed as many positive responses from special students to various questions as were given by the nonretarded. Special class students do reject the stigma of special placement but hold many positive attitudes toward their classroom and school experiences.

Martin, Edwin W.: Individualism and behaviorism as future trends in educating handicapped children. *Except Child,* 38:7, 517-525, March 1972.

Special education has always been focused on the individual. The strategies for achieving this goal continue to evolve, but the predominant strategy today is to reduce the complexity of teaching handicapped children. Using labels has proved less efficient than expected, so an exploration of another system of categorization is needed, that is, the relevant behaviors of the child.

A new emphasis on the individual is developing and will become more pronounced in the next decade. Teacher education programs are taking new form, reducing categorical approaches, exploring diagnostic and resource roles in addition to classroom teaching roles. These are attempts to respond to the needs of the child rather than his disability. Teachers are too often insensitive to the feelings of the children or the parents with whom they are working.

Reimbursement systems are now being developed in several states making possible the financial support of special education programs without the usual close ties to the labeling process. It seems likely that we will one day see the growth of this type of administrative flexibility which will allow many more handicapped children to participate in the regular school program.

Rapier, Jacqueline, Adelson, Ruth, Carey, Richard, and Croke, Katherine: Changes in children's attitudes toward the physically handicapped. *Except Child*, 39:3, 219-223, Nov. 1972.

The article reports the results of an assessment which was made of changes in attitude of 152 elementary school children toward orthopedically handicapped children as a result of an integrated school experience. After integration, nonhandicapped children had developed a more positive attitude toward the handicapped. The findings indicate the importance of administrators providing favorable interactions between orthopedically handicapped children and nonhandicapped children.

Reger, Roger: Case study of the effects of labeling: Funding and provision of services. *Journal of Learning Disabilities*, 7:10, 650-651, Dec. 1974.

The appropriateness and relevance of labeling are discussed by the author. There are two types of labeling brought out in the article: 1) labeling of the student, and 2) labeling of the program. With all the pros and cons considered, labeling is about the only way that special programs are funded. No matter if labeling is liked or disliked, it appears to be the price one must pay for obtaining funds for programs for special needs students.

Simches, Raphael F.: The inside outsiders. *Except Child*, 37:1, 5-15, Sept. 1970.

The author discusses the positive and negative aspects of special education today:

Positive: 1) no longer a problem of legislation; 2) rapid development of instructional media; 3) regionalization of low incidence handicaps; 4) operant conditioning becoming a prime factor in special education programs; 5) growth of parent operated programs for the handicapped; 6) new emphasis on individualized instruction; 7) new educational technologies.

Negative: 1) utilization of research—or lack thereof; 2) teacher training; 3) implementation of legislation; 4) maximizing of options for programs; 5) labeling and identification of children.

LEGISLATION

Abeson, Alan, and Trudeau, Elaine: Handicapped children redefined—Legal eligibility for services expanded. *Except Child,* 37:4, 305-311, Dec. 1970.

Laws are increasing the range of exceptional children eligible for special education services.

Eliminate age six as earliest age of entry.

Extend limit from eighteen to twenty-one years and in some cases twenty-four years.

More than half of the states authorize programs for the handicapped until age twenty-one.

Increasing awareness of the "learning disabled" child.

An overview of the definitions of the handicapped and the age requirements for programs in fifty states. (Listed Michigan as having no maximum or minimum age.)

Collection of information was for purpose of analyzing, summarizing, and disseminating information to special educators for decision makers and other interested persons.

Abeson, Alan: Movement and momentum: Government and the education of handicapped children. *Except Child,* 39:1, 63-66, Sept. 1972.

Within the past year, a general movement is occurring at all levels of government—attorney general's rulings, state and federal legislation— the viewing of an education for handicapped as an "inalienable" right.

In the past few years many states gave schools the option of serving the handicapped. Now, about 70 percent of the states have passed mandatory education laws. Also lowering of eligibility age to birth and in some cases raising it to twenty-five.

A new subcommittee of the Senate Labor and Welfare Committee, called the Subcommittee for the Handicapped is indicative of a new awareness at the federal level.

The activity of the nation's courts must be mentioned. Implicit in the litigation movement is the idea that handicapped individuals, even though institutionalized, have the right to an education. Policy makers must be aware of this fact and must act. Many groups not traditionally concerned with the handicapped are now becoming involved.

The real test at this point is that special education communities must be prepared to provide quality education for all handicapped children—programs which will not only teach children, but will stand the test of accountability.

Carey, Hugh: Educational services for the handicapped: Federal role. *Compact,* 5:4, 8-13, Aug. 1971.

Since 1957, federal funds have only provided models of educational programs for the handicapped. The purpose of these model programs is to initiate interest and funds at the state and local levels.

Carey is promoting a federal allocation of funds to provide up to one third of the excess cost of educating a handicapped child.

This federal provision for basic support in the education of handicapped youngsters would result in a more adequate implementation in all areas of educational services to the handicapped.

Dukakis, Michael S.: It's the law. *The Exceptional Parent,* 1:2, 28-31, Sept. 1971.

This is a section of the new magazine for parents of the exceptional child. Their aim is to bring before the parents legislation which will contribute to the services for their children. In this specific article, they addressed it to the specific stages in the legislative procedures and how a bill becomes a law. The other aspect covered was citizen involvement in lobbying. The article was in laymen's vernacular and thus very readable for the average parent.

Hensley, Gene: Special education: No longer handicapped. *Compact,* 7:4, 3-5, Oct. 1973.

The overview presented by the author covered many trends in the education of the handicapped. State legislation was reviewed and a graph of states and percentages of the handicapped they serve was presented. As the result of important court decisions, programs for the handicapped are being established. The only drawback to the current movement of educating the handicapped is the lack of funds and teacher shortages in some states.

Irvin, Thomas B.: Assistance to states for education of handicapped children under ESEA Title VI-A. *Except Child, 34*:7, 565-568, March 1968.

This article describes types of activities and services available for special education in the states. Support can be secured for, a) qualified leadership personnel, b) special teachers and teacher aides in all disabilities, c) other related personnel such as therapists, psychologists, social workers, etc. The article also describes services such as work study programs, special transportation arrangements, mobile units, instructional materials, and remodeling of classrooms and diagnostic services.

Mackie, Romaine: The handicapped benefit under compensatory education programs. *Except Child, 34*:8, 603-608, April 1968.

The author cites the benefits to handicapped children which are to be gained through participation in programs funded under Title I of the Elementary and Secondary Education Act of 1965. They are: Encompassing handicapped children who are victims of their environment; preventing and reversing conditions for those who suffer from environmental and cultural deprivation; funds going directly to school districts; exploring the overlap of mental retardation and cultural deprivation.

Martin, Edwin: Breakthrough for the handicapped: Legislative history. *Except Child, 34*:7, 493-503, March 1968.

The article deals with the federal laws regarding cooperative research, captioned films for the deaf and amendments to Title VI of ESEA. Each law is fully explained. The final meaning of the legislation and fulfillment of its promise lie in the efforts of professionals to give handicapped children a chance at a better life through their successful work with them.

Martin, Edwin W.: Bureau of education for the handicapped commitment and program in early childhood education. *Except Child, 37*:9, 661-663, May 1971.

The author reports that the development of preschool programs for the handicapped has been inhibited not only by lack of support but by the paucity of model or prototype programs which could provide the basis for local planning and by the lack of structured information on the factors making for success in early intervention with handicapped children. This extent of unmet needs prompted the Handicapped Children's Early Education Assistance Act in 1968 which is intended to be catalytic by stimulating local and state efforts by demonstrating its effectiveness of early childhood education and by giving visibility to such programs. The main objective is to provide equal educational opportunities to every child and it is felt that preschool programming is essential to this goal.

Martin, Edwin, Jr., LaVor, Martin, Bryan, Trudy, and Scheflin, Rhona: P.L. 91-230, The Elementary and Secondary Education Act Amendments of 1969: Title VI, The Education of the Handicapped Act. *Except Child,* 37:1, 53-56, Summer 1970.

On April 13, 1970, President Nixon signed into law P.L. 91-230, the Elementary and Secondary Education Act Amendments of 1969 (ESEA) cementing newly created and existing legislation into a single statute to insure efficient administration of the many programs for the handicapped. It increased authorization from $320 million to $486 million by 1973.

Martin, Edwin W.: New public priority: Education of the handicapped. *Compact,* 5:4, 4-7, Aug. 1971.

Sidney P. Marland has called for a national goal of full educational opportunity for all handicapped children by 1980.

Support for the goal can be derived from these facts: 1) Educating the handicapped is successful, and 2) their education saves dollars as opposed to services they may later require because of educational deprivation.

In order to achieve this goal it will be necessary to have a joint commitment by all agencies and the cooperation and combined support among the agencies toward the commitments. Also, federal financial funds must aid in providing a substantial amount of basic support.

Ross, Sterling, DeYoung, Henry, and Cohen, Julius: Confrontation: Special education and the law. *Except Child,* 38:1, 5-12, Sept. 1971.

A review of various court suits dealing with the rights of children to be included in special education or to be excluded from such programs.

The authors indicated that many EMR classes are unwitting burial grounds for children from environments that have not prepared them for the demands of the school. The following reasons are developed:

1) Testing does not accurately measure the learning ability. 2) The administration of tests is too often performed incompetently. 3) Parents are not given an adequate chance to participate in placement. 4) Special Education programming is often inadequate and becomes a self-fulfilling negative concept by leaving the student there. 5)Irreparable personal harm is often created by improper placement.

Recent cases have forced compensation for damages to be given and insisted that parents must have prior hearings and notice before official labels are given. The authors conclude that pathology may reside, not in the child, but in the school or university training of educators and psychologists. Our need is for a careful reexamination of behavior of school staff rather than of children. People, not systems, hurt other people.

Special Report, Newly funded demonstration grants for improved learning disabilities services. *Journal of Learning Disabilities*, 5:10, 57-62, Dec. 1972.

This article is a special report giving information about new Child Service Demonstration Programs funded under Title VI of ESEA. Their purpose is to improve education for the handicapped. The report gives information on each program being set up in fifteen different states.

PROGRAM TRENDS

Christoplos, Florence: Keeping exceptional children in regular classes. *Except Child*, 39:7, 569-572, April 1973.

The author gives a list of reasons for supporting integration of handicapped children into regular classrooms. They are: 1) financial necessity, 2) disappointing results from segregated classes, 3) need for developing respect for individual differences, 4) detrimental effects on exceptional children's egos, 5) need for mutual self respect and consideration, 6) need to develop curricula removed from artificial norms, and 7) meaningful appreciation of ethnic, racial, sexual, physical, and ability variations without judgments. Cristoplos describes a pilot project funded by U.S.O.E., B.E.H. designed to help regular class teachers manage the problems created by having one type of handicapped child integrated into their regular classes.

Haring, Norris G., and Krug, David A.: Placement in regular programs. *Except Child,* 41:6, 413-418, March, 1975.

Forty-eight mentally impaired students of elementary age who lived in a disadvantaged area were selected at random. All were divided and matched into experimental and control groups. The objective was to initiate an experimental individualized instruction program that would facilitate the return to regular classes. Results showed that a high percentage could acquire basic skills to allow regular class placement.

Martin, Edwin M.: Some thoughts on mainstreaming. *Except Child,* 41:3, 150-154, Nov. 1974.

Martin, who is in charge of the Bureau for Education of the Handicapped, U.S.O.E. discusses some of the issues faced in implementing the concept of "mainstreaming" handicapped children. He cautions that if mainstreaming is treated as an educational fad, without examining the underlying philosophical and educational foundation, then it is doomed to failure. He points out the need to reexamine teacher education, educational planning, and the need for a more effective evaluation of all work being done with the handicapped.

Melcher, John W.: Some questions from a school administrator. *Except Child,* 38:7, 547-551, March 1972.

In this succinct statement, a number of contemporary issues in special education are discussed. The current trend toward mainstreaming exceptional learners is the primary point of interest. In considering this point, several related items such as the role of state/federal agencies, legislation and universities are also discussed. The author discusses the dilemma facing classroom teachers and administrators who have not been trained to deal with exceptional learners. Finally the need for more comprehensive teacher training programs is reviewed.

Shotel, Jay, Iano, Richard, and McGettigan, James: Teacher attitudes associated with the integration of handicapped children. *Except Child,* 38:9, 677-683, May 1972.

The authors describe how regular classroom teachers felt about the integration of handicapped persons into the regular classroom. This would be the situation where resource rooms are used.

Teachers found that EMR students did not integrate well academically and socially into their regular classrooms even though they had support from a resource teacher. This suggests that a reorganization of elementary school programs into a non-graded pattern with flexible placement is needed if EMR students are to be successful in general education. Teachers were found to be more positive toward the integration of emotionally disturbed children than with the EMR children.

If regular teachers do not think they can teach handicapped children, then it is unrealistic to expect them to accept the responsibility with confidence. If these students are to be integrated, the following services are necessary for the regular teachers: 1) the need for inservice workshops on methods and techniques, 2) an opportunity to observe resource rooms in action, and 3) a provision for intensive communication and interaction among resource and regular class teachers.

PROGRAM OPERATION

Anderson, Kathryn A.: The "shopping" behavior of parents of mentally retarded children: The professional person's role. *Ment Retard*, 9:4, 3-5, Aug. 1971.

The diagnostic and therapeutic "shopping" of parents of retarded children is described as a learned response to unsatisfactory contacts with professional people regarding their child. The role of the professional person in initiating or preventing and in stopping shopping behavior is discussed with special emphasis on the informing interview. The need for research in this area is underscored, and areas for research are suggested.

Austin, James T.: Video-tape as a teaching tool. *Except Child*, 35:7, 557-558, March 1969.

Austin reports that he initially utilized the video recording system as a tool to help modify the attitudes of persons working with retarded individuals. It was found that video-taping stimulated creative teaching and helped the teachers develop a greater awareness of their interaction with students.

Teachers would tape complete classes and would evaluate their effectiveness. Teachers who felt hesitant about the video-taping were permitted to view their tapes privately for up to two months; they were then required to share them and permit group evaluation.

The video-tape also was found to have a positive effect on the students. They were able to view their interaction and view themselves as others do. It was also found that some students lost enthusiasm and felt that they were making little progress; tapes of past and present abilities constituted visual proof of progress.

Video-tapes were also used in training aides, university students and volunteers. Parents, during conferences, were able to view their child. As a public relations method, the video-tapes were excellent.

Barngrover, Elaine: A study of educators' preference in special education programs. *Except Child,* 37:10, 754-755, Summer 1971.

In 1970, fifty teachers, administrators and school psychologists were interviewed to determine if they felt that special classes for the EMR child are presently able to fill his needs or if he would be better served by being returned to the more heterogeneous grouping of the regular classroom. Twenty-seven felt that the present program of providing special classes should be retained. Reasons cited were: less disruption in the regular classroom, more success for the EMR child, more individual attention, specialized help for special deficits, and more realistic preparation for the working world. Improvements suggested were more qualified teachers, more and better materials, smaller classes, curriculum more suited to the child's needs, and more integration into the school's activities.

The most frequent reasons in support of the position taken by the twenty-three interviewees who advocated placement in the regular classroom included widened horizons and greater stimulation for the special child in heterogeneous groupings, more good peer behavior models to emulate and more group pressure toward good behavior, higher expectations of progress in a regular class, and the failure of present special classes to meet special needs. Provisions most frequently suggested were smaller classes; team teaching; flexibility of grouping, grading, and scheduling; individualization of instruction; and the availability of special help from resource and crisis teachers, counselors, psychologists, and learning diagnosticians.

Baumgartner, Bernice, and Lynch, Katherine D.: Administering classes for the retarded: What kinds of principals and supervisors are needed. *Except Child*, 34:2, 51-52, Oct. 1967.

This is a book review which deals vividly with the concept that administrators and regular schools are not relieved of the responsibility of special education programs. The theme of the book is one of continuity of programming for the mentally retarded. Chapters are devoted to selection of teachers, principal's role in working with supervision, school environment, in-service education, and working with parents. The reviewer feels the book's usefulness to qualified directors is in question. The book's value would seem more useful to schools which are in the beginning stages of program planning for the retarded.

Bentovim, Arnon: Disturbed and under five. *Spec Educ*, 62:2, 31-35, June 1973.

Although the author describes a program in operation in London, there are ideas which can be applied to the United States. The program involves a day care center for preschool emotionally disturbed children and their parents. The plan is to provide more than the traditional out-patient child guidance clinician. The staff, including social workers and psychiatrists, work with parents and children for an entire day, several times weekly. After three years, the center has seen success and continues to conduct research on improving methodology.

Blessing, Kenneth (Ed.): *The Role of the Resource Consultant*. Council for Exceptional Children Monograph, Washington, D.C., 1-127, 1968.

The monograph is a statement of the role of resource consultants with the various types of handicapped children. Each chapter was written by a professional who is recognized as an expert in a specific area of the handicapped.

Bloch, Judith: A preschool workshop for emotionally disturbed children. *Children, 17*:1, 10-14, January-February 1973.

The author describes a school for emotionally disturbed children of preschool and kindergarten age. The object of the experience given the children was to improve their level of functioning so that they could attend school or at least avoid institutionalization. The major approach to assisting the children in this setting is "intrusion," or placing contingencies on the child's behavior, thus forcing him to face reality. The approach was apparently successful.

Brolin, Donn: Career education needs of secondary educable students. *Except Child, 39*:8, 619-624, May 1973.

The article identifies the instructional needs of junior and senior high educable mentally handicapped students and the competencies teachers must have to meet those needs. It further identifies the other types of personnel who should be involved in working with handicapped youngsters at this level.

It was noted that special education teachers are still trained to teach primarily academic skills, and that they place great emphasis on purely academic instruction while neglecting vocational evaluation, work adjustment, placement techniques, and other career areas. The author also points out the weakness in communication between the classroom teacher and the vocational education instructor and/or the vocational rehabilitation counselor.

Bullock, Lyndal, and Whelan, Richard: Competencies needed by teachers of the emotionally disturbed and socially maladjusted: A comparison. *Except Child, 37*:7, 485-489, March 1971.

One of the most comprehensive attempts to determine competencies of teachers of emotionally disturbed children was conducted by Mackie, Kvaraceus, and Williams (1957). A list of eighty-eight competencies was compiled and 147 teachers of the disturbed were asked to rate the importance of each competency, using a four point scale. Forty-seven teachers of the disturbed in a midwestern state were asked to complete the same checklist in order to assess how teachers currently involved in the education of the disturbed viewed the competencies which had been delimited earlier. Information obtained from the current group of teachers was compared to the original Mackie et al. study. The present inquiry showed that teachers of the disturbed considered very important only 12 of the 88 competencies. Of the twelve, only five were also considered very important by the teachers in the study conducted by Mackie et al. From the data analysis and the information provided by the five competencies, both groups saw as very important some suggestions for teacher preparation in this field. They were as follows: 1) A need to place renewed emphasis on individualized and sequential programming techniques in order to ensure school success, 2) the need to provide teachers with a working knowledge of the education and psychology of the various types of exceptional children, 3) a need to train teachers to perform through a multidisciplinary approach, 4) the need of a thorough knowledge of behavioral principles as they apply to the management of these children.

Calovini, Gloria: *The Principal Looks at Classes for the Physically Handicapped.* Council for Exceptional Children Monograph, Washington, D.C., 1969.

Calovini gives a brief overview of programs for the physically handicapped and provides practical suggestions for principals who may have such programs in their buildings. The appendices contain a brief description of the most commonly found physical handicaps and the organizations and agencies which deal with them.

Changing Times: Cheaper ways to build schools. *The Kiplinger Magazine,* Oct., 1971.

This article introduces the reader to a number of trends in school construction methods that are saving money, not always spectacular amounts, but enough to help many districts hold the line against rising costs.

The suggestions are as follows: 1) Use of the systems approach to building—prefabricated units, etc. 2) Set up time schedules—pert chart. 3) Do not build walls—use of flexible open spaces. 4) Rent the air, share the land—build schools on the first levels of high rises. 5) Look around—convert existing sound structures.

Cogen, Victor, and Ohrtman, William F.: A comprehensive plan for services to the handicapped. *Journal of Special Education,* 5:1, 73-79, Winter-Spring 1971.

The authors state that services for the handicapped are provided by a variety of sources; private, public comprehensive, and/or limited with serious overlap and gaps. They suggest a model based on voluntary cooperation of all agencies in a state. The model consists of nine segments or areas: 1) genetic counseling, 2) prenatal care, 3) early identification, 4) diagnosis, 5) care and custody, 6) preschool programs, 7) primary education, 8) intermediate education (prevocational included), and 9) community programs.

The authors propose that a continuous and computerized record system be used, with common terminology so that gaps in service can be identified and closed.

Cormay, Robert B.: Returning special education students to regular classes. *Personnel and Guidance Journal,* 48:8, 641-646, April 1970.

Generally, placement of students in special education classes has been a one-way street. While many students are placed in special education classes each year, few are returned to regular classes. This study investigated the effects of being returned to regular classes on thirty special education students. The results showed that special education students, given proper screening and orientation, can be returned to regular classes and show academic and social success.

While this study was primarily interested in the role of the counselor in successful reverse placement, it has considerable significance for the special education administrator. The new state guidelines and regulations regarding special class placement make it imperative that the special education administrator take effective steps towards returning special education students to regular classes. To make this transition less traumatic for the student, the administrator should keep in mind what successful reverse placement entails. This is indicated in the study.

Dearth, Beverly, J., Kingsley, Ronald J., and Laughton, Reginald: Teacher supervisory functions in TMR programs. *Ment Retard,* 9:5, 41-43, Oct. 1971.

A survey was undertaken to compare the perception of administrators and teachers in viewing the issues related to teacher/ supervisor functions in community class programs for the TMR. This survey gave evidence concerning recommendations for educational procedures and practices. Divergent reporting was seen, however, between administrators' and teachers' perceptions of existing educational procedures and practices. These differing perceptions may suggest problem areas which deserve attention. The technique of comparing views and perceptions utilized in this study may suggest a procedure having wide applicability in uncovering problem areas in educational programs, generally.

DeMichael, Salvator G.: Providing full vocational opportunities for retarded adolescents. *The Digest of the Mentally Retarded*, 3:1, 56-62, Fall 1966.

The plan makes it possible for every mentally retarded adolescent to have continuous opportunity to develop work skills, consistent with his level of ability, interests, and personal-social attributes. Each person working in the program progresses through successive levels according to his probable work placement.

Divoky, Diane: Education's latest victim: The "L.D." kid. *Learning, The Magazine for Creative Thinking*, 3:2, 20-25, Oct. 1974.

Divoky explores the concept that nearly every child who displays an atypical behavior, e.g. stuttering, digestive problems, bed-wetting, hair twirling, masturbating, "scatterbrained," overly-talkative, reading problems, writing problems, is one who is learning disabled. She is concerned with evermounting statistics indicating that the learning disabled are whomever the diagnosticians want them to be. The label seems to put the blame for the children's problems on no one, not the family, the children, the school, or society. It seems to diminish the feeling of guilt for all concerned and offers a reasonable rationale for failure. No one can be held responsible for neurological conditions. The inference of some type of minimal brain pathology or impairment is a reassuring concept for parents and teachers in need of an explanation for the problems their children are exhibiting, that is, overactivity, underactivity, distractibility, emotional instability, or poor coordination.

Douglas, Joseph H.: A "new thrust" approach to mental retardation. *Am J Ment Def*, 76:2, 145-152, Sept. 1971.

"New Thrust" is predicated upon a) the knowledge that from 75 to 85 percent of the retarded show no demonstrable physiological damage and b) the assumption that the societal and environmental aspects of mental retardation, though perhaps less precise or dramatic must be considered in planning their education.

The most fruitful attack for prevention and positive modification in the future seems to lie with the following: a) Biology and environment do not work independently of each other, b) efforts to disentangle the various influences and to understand their interaction, c) redefinition of the developmental potential of the retarded in positive terms, and d) establish approaches based on research.

Dunn, Lloyd: Special education for the mildly retarded—Is much of it justifiable? *Except Child,* 35:1, 5-22, Sept. 1968.

Segregated programs for the mildly handicapped are unjust in that they may violate the children's civil rights. Such classrooms relate to tracking which is still under fire from a civil rights point of view.

Research has shown that the mildly retarded do as well or better when in hetrogeneous groupings and do not suffer from labeling. The new direction seems to be toward team teaching, nongraded schools and more specialized personnel, along with more sophisticated equipment. The trend is toward a clinical approach, with special education teachers more in the role of diagnosis and prescription, with the special class itself serving as a resource room.

Special education needs to become an integral part of a whole community improvement agency. Working in such an agency, more could be done to improve the environment of all underprivileged children.

The program must go deeper into specific learning disabilities. Sensory and perceptual training in the auditory and visual skills, as well as language and speech development constitute the bulk of the training program. The program must also put emphasis on personality, social interaction and vocational development and training.

Eagle, Edward: Prognosis and outcome of community placement of institutionalized retardates. *Am J Ment Def*, 72:2, 232-243, Sept. 1967.

There are questions as to the outcome of taking institutionalized clients and placing them in homes. Problems arise from limited amount of supervision and guidance of discharged patients, excessive case loads preventing adequate follow-up work, and vocational placement. This is usually relegated to local welfare agencies which are already overworked. Of 7436 released, 39.6 percent had an unfavorable prognosis. More research and critical evaluation of placement procedures are needed.

Englehardt, George M.: Increasing the efficacy of special class placement for the socially maladjusted. *J of Spec Ed*, 4:4, 441-444, Fall-Winter 1970.

The author quotes those who say that special education programs for the mentally handicapped have failed to prove their worth. The author believes that if a testing procedure could be used to give the child exactly what he needs—educational, therapeutic, or other services—the programs would be more successful.

The problem of early identification is crucial. A sample of non-rehabilitants (mean age 9.38) and a sample from a rehabilitation center were examined. The hypothesis was that there would be no discrimination possible between rehabilitated and nonrehabilitated groups of socially maladjusted boys. The hypothesis was rejected on the basis of a 75 percent accurate rate in identification at the time of placement.

Farley, Gordan, and Godard, Lenore: Sex education of E.D. children with learning disorders. *J of Sp Ed*, 4:4, 445-450, Winter 1970.

The authors made connections between inhibitions related to learning about the human body and learning inhibitions in general. They also suggested a curriculum for use in this area.

Frankel, Harold, and Bateman, Barbara: Special education and the pediatrician. *J of Learn Disabil*, 5:4, 178-186, April 1972.

This article deals with the involvement of the pediatrician in educational planning of exceptional children. The article discusses areas of mutual interest to educators and doctors of pediatric medicine. These areas include mental retardation, learning disabilities, reading problems and parent groups. It goes on to discuss some of the emerging trends in special education and the pediatrician's involvement in these trends. The article concludes by listing three specific steps the pediatrician involved in special education might follow. They are: 1) know the special education personnel and services in your locale; 2) adopt a "problem area" philosophy which enables the physicians' primary responsibility to be delivery of medical services; 3) lend support to that within the special education world which is helpful and at the same time assist in making changes where they are needed.

Gallagher, James J.: Organization and special education. *Except Child*, 34:7, 485-491, March 1968.

The job of all educators, including special educators, is to find the mechanisms through which we can translate new knowledge into action at the instructional level. The author indicates that there are five major states in the knowledge to action cycle: research, development, demonstration, implementation, and adoption.

We achieve implementation of programs with the highly sophisticated and complex society . . . through complex systems and organizations. Our goal for handicapped children is self-realization and self-sufficiency.

The Bureau for the Education of the Handicapped is both a symbol of that determination and a vehicle whereby such a realization can more easily be obtained.

Gallagher, James J.: The special education contract for mildly handicapped children. *Except Child*, 38:7, 527-535, March 1972.

This article is concerned with two issues: 1) The difficulty of replacement of mildly handicapped children in regular education after they have been in special education and 2) the high percentage of certain minority group children in special education.

The author has suggested a special education contract for mildly retarded, disturbed, or learning disabled children. This contract would be signed by parents and educators, with specific goals and a clear time limit to reach these goals. The maximum time limit for the contract would be two years.

The contract would give specific objectives for the child and would be upgraded at six-month intervals. Through this contract the following would be obtained: 1) Parents would be aware of placement and objectives. 2) The child would know that he would be returning to a regular classroom and that he was expected to meet certain objectives. 3) Regular education would know that it would have the child back in two years or less and they would have to plan for a program when he returned. 4) Special educators would have to put forth maximum effort so the child would be ready to return to the regular class. 5) Parents would know that the school was giving a special two-year effort to help their child prepare for later educational goals.

Garrison, Mortimer Jr.: The perceived adequacy of programming in mental retardation. *Ment Retard*, 8:1, 2-5, Feb. 1970.

The results of a questionnaire are reported in this article. The questionnaire was sent to 3,000 persons directly or indirectly involved with programs for the retarded. The President's Committee on Mental Retardation used this questionnaire to assist in ascertaining the adequacy of programs for the retarded. The most significant result found by this questionnaire is the fact that so many persons appeared not to be informed about programs and services for the retarded. Variations in adequacy are seen and all programs need improvement. The author suggests using the American Association for Mental Deficiency standards as models.

Garrison, Mortimer Jr., and Hammill, Donald: Who are the retarded? *Except Child*, 38:1, 13-20, Sept. 1971.

This study was designed to investigate the validity of special class placements by comparing children enrolled in educable classes with their peers in regular classes by using multiple criteria.

The educable class is usually designed to provide a developmental program with goals of job success and social adequacy in adulthood. It is generally not remedial in its philosophy. The findings of this study suggest that 25 percent of the children found in the EMR classes may be misplaced.

The class for educable should be provided for those who will benefit from it. Others need opportunities offered through a resource room, tutoring, nongraded classes, or a learning center approach. These programs focus on remediating deficiencies or teaching needed skills so that the child can be integrated into the regular school class.

Glaser, William: The effect of school failure. *Educational Digest,* 35:4, 13-17, Dec. 1969.

Children who are labeled as failures also behave that way. Labels are usually euphemisms for failure. Each child needs to have a unique identity. Love is a success pathway to a child. Success as a goal for children should be the top priority for schools and this must begin with the administration and permeate all staff.

Glass, Raymond, and Roy Mechlen: Preparing elementary teachers to instruct mildly handicapped children in regular classrooms; A summer workshop. *Except Child,* 39:2, 152-156, Oct. 1972.

In Indiana in the summer of 1971, eighteen elementary teachers participated in a workshop. The major goals of the workshop were to equip elementary teachers with the diagnostic, remedial, and behavior management skills that would increase their ability to successfully instruct mildly handicapped children in regular classrooms.

In the area of attitudes and beliefs it appears that participants viewed themselves as more competent to teach mildly handicapped children, and more attracted to having them in their regular education classes.

The authors indicated that this is a more productive procedure for teaching these skills than the traditional university courses.

Glavin, John, Quay, Herbert, Annesley, Frederick, and Werry, John: An experimental resource room for behavior problem children. *Except Child,* 38:2, 131-137, Oct. 1971.

The Temple Resource Room project attempted an alternative to the self-contained classroom for the behaviorally disoriented of twenty-seven elementary children. Fourteen attended the resource room two periods a day, eleven for one period in reading, two for one period in arithmetic. Responsibility for the child remained with the regular class teacher. Poker chips were used as secondary reinforcers, converted later to cards and objects. The staff received training.

The effect of resource rooms on academic achievement was encouraging. There was also a decrease in deviant behavior.

Granger, Ben P.: Dilemmas of re-organizing institutions for the mentally retarded. *Ment Retard, 10*:4, 3-7, Aug. 1972.

The author states that reform is necessary in the pattern of care for the mentally retarded. He quotes Wolfesberger and others as experts. Often comprehensive planning is done, but the implementation is left to chance. A study of two state institutions was conducted as they were reorganizing according to a "unitization" plan. Both were relative failures and met with resistance by direct care personnel. The patients noticed little or no difference.

Alternative innovation is really making the unitization a reality by involving patients and staff in planning and implementation; however, the author feels that it is "too little, too late." He proposes a system called Community-based Services with a life style of all mentally retarded persons to be as normal as possible. Living would range from private homes, hostels, and community residences to general hospitals for those who need special care. This would necessarily mean the community would be involved and the lives of the mentally retarded would be more consistent with a free society instead of "warehousing" or institutionalizing as is now generally accepted in the United States.

Greenspan, Stanley, and Horvath, Richard: A public school program of economic independence for special education students. *Am Ann of the Deaf, 118*:5, 567-584, Oct. 1973.

The authors describe a plan currently in operation in California which provides handicapped students with a goal upon high school termination. Prevocational information is made available to students from preschool through grade eight. The program cited deals with hearing impaired children. Their high school program is very carefully planned and guided by teachers and other specialists. The ultimate goal of such a program is to enable handicapped young people to become self-sufficient and economically independent people.

Guerin, Gilbert R.: Special classes or resource rooms? *Ment Retard,* 5:1, 40-41, Feb. 1967.

To facilitate better educational experiences for the EMR and to prepare him for life in the community, two alternatives are offered—special classes or resource rooms. Since it is believed that education is restricted by segregation, recent stress is toward integrating the EMR into regular classes at both the elementary and secondary levels. In the resource program, the integration would be partial; a committee would make assignments and also decide amount of time and subject(s) to be taught. Realistic goals would be set (slow growth should be expected), and regular classroom and resource teachers could work together to provide the necessary flexibility.

Guerin, Gilbert, and Szatlocky, Kathleen: Integration programs for the mildly retarded. *Except Child,* 41:3, 173-179, Nov. 1974.

The authors report a study that examined programs which integrate mentally retarded students into regular classrooms in California. A variety of program procedures were found to be used when integrating educable mentally retarded students into regular classrooms. The majority of the teaching staff approved of the integration and were supported in their attitudes by both their central office and building administrators.

Guralnick, Michael J.: A language development program for severely handicapped children. *Except Child,* 39:1, 45-49, Sept. 1972.

This article describes a program for severely handicapped children designed to be conducted by college students. It is based on behavioral principles and is intended to develop verbal behavior in the handicapped children. The results of the program showed that the college students were able to make important contributions to the language development of the severely handicapped children. Their success was attributed to their technical skills obtained mainly from the increasing number of behaviorally oriented undergraduate courses now being offered. The findings of the study have important implications in light of the shortage of technical personnel in institutions and treatment centers.

Hall, Sylvia M., and Talkington, Larry W.: Trends in programming for deaf mentally retarded in public residential facilities. *Ment Retard, 10*:2, 50-52, April, 1972.

A survey of programs available for the deaf mentally retarded in state public residential schools for the deaf and public institutions for the mentally retarded is reported in this paper. Method: A postcard questionnaire was sent to all sixty-two state public residential schools for the deaf and all 169 public institutions for the mentally retarded in the United States. The questionnaire covered the following questions: 1) Do you have a special program for the deaf M.R.? 2) Number of DMR? 3) Criteria used to classify deaf? 4) Criteria used to classify M.R.? 5) Is your program run by a teacher of the deaf or teacher of the mentally retarded?

Findings—A lack of personnel trained to work with dual handicap of deafness and retardation is apparent. New approaches for the establishment of special training programs for DMR need to be considered. Personnel presently working with DMR need to effect program evaluation efforts regarding the results of techniques and methodologies applicable to such programming. A more unified effort between schools for the deaf and institutions for the mentally retarded is needed in planning programs for individual DMR who do not readily fit into current programs. Better communications and exchange of program information must be facilitated. A special emphasis may be needed on program development for the DMR who falls below the mild to borderline level of retardation.

Harring, Norris, and Krug, David: Placement in regular programs: Procedures and results. *Except Child, 41*:6, 413-417, March 1975.

The authors reported a study which was initiated in order to gain information which would help provide information needed for mainstreaming the handicapped into regular classrooms. These pupils were from low socio-economic areas who had been placed in classes for the educable mentally retarded. The results showed that the majority of the students could acquire basic skills at a rate to allow regular class placement.

Hoeltke, Gary M.: Effectiveness of special class placement. Paper presented to the 91st annual meeting of the American Association on Mental Deficiency, Denver, Col., May 15-20, 1967.

The effectiveness of special class placement of EMR children was evaluated in terms of self-concept, attitude toward the teacher, academic achievement, social maturity, and behavioral development. Twenty-five EMR's in special classes in Iowa were matched with twenty-five EMR controls on IQ as determined on either the S-B or WISC, CA and sex. The control group or regular class sample was selected from districts where there was no program or an extremely limited one. All S's in the experimental group had been in special class programs for three or more years and resided in districts where most EMR's were placed in special classes. The WRAT, Vineland SMS, and scales developed to measure attitudes toward teachers, self-concept, and behavioral development were employed for assessment. The Wilcoxon Matched Pairs Test was used to test for significance of the difference between sample scores. Data indicated that special class students held a more positive self-concept than children in regular classes, but regular class children learned more reading, spelling, and arithmetic as measured on the tests. Sex of the enrollee was not a significant factor. The children in both classes showed the same attitude toward their teachers.

Hollinger, S. Chloe, and Jones, Reginald L.: Community attitudes toward slow learners and mental retardates: What's in a name. *Ment Retard*, 8:1, 19-24, Feb. 1970.

One hundred-fourteen randomly selected residents of a small Ohio community responded to informational and attitudinal questionnaires regarding the terms "mental retardation" and "slow learner." The results revealed that the general public had many misconceptions concerning these labels. Generally, "slow learners" was a term of greater acceptance while "mental retardate" was thought of as emotionally impaired.

Ishiaq, Kishwar: Counseling the parents of retarded children. *Ment Retard*, 10:5, 501, Oct. 1972.

The author discusses the need for parent counseling services. Group therapy and parent associations are both effective methods used. Parents of mentally retarded children need to be heard and understood so that they can cope with their problems and help their child to adjust.

Jones, Reginald: Accountability in special education. *Except Child,* 39:8, 631-642, May 1973.

The main thrust of the article is concerned with the problems associated with "outcome accountability" in which teachers are responsible to the school district management for producing program outcomes consistent with preselected objectives of a performance standard appropriate for the instructional program. The essential notion underlying outcome accountability is that if professional education can be held responsible for educational outcomes, favorable changes will be reflected in higher academic achievement, improved pupil attitudes, and generally better results. Accountability in special education must be preceded by considerable conceptualizing at administrative, school board, and public levels and that the burden should not be placed directly on teachers.

Jorgensen, I. Skov: Special education in the rehabilitation program. U.S. Dept. of Health, Education and Welfare, Office of Education, Aug. 1968, 1-43.

The author's thesis is that special education is prescribed education and that the prescription is derived from the pupil's own requirements. In Sweden, counselors arrange for instruction with a pronounced occupational bias during the last few years of schooling. The idea of special education is to compensate for defects and build on strengths, choosing a placement that is satisfactory and at the same time requiring as little uprooting as possible.

Jubenville, Charles P.: Programming for severely mentally retarded. Mental Retardation: Selected Conference Papers, Springfield, Ill., Illinois Mental Health Department, 1969, pp. 40-46.

The goals and objectives of programs for SMR's should be habit formation and socialization. Individual training programs should have short- and long-range goals, and these programs should be based on a complete social history, medical evaluation and history, and psychological evaluation. Activities related to short-range goals should be designed so that they build toward the long-range goals. Short-range goals should be stressed in the child's daily training program. The environment should be conducive to training activities, the environment for the young SMR's should be highly structured. Sedentary and physical activities should alternate at frequent intervals. The principles of persistence, consistency, and continuity are vital to a habit development program. When children's maturation and readiness for a more complex activity is noted, it should be introduced. The progress of SMR's in a group training program should be evaluated so that parents can be informed about progress and decisions about new programs, program emphasis, and procedures can be made.

Kaplan, Bert L.: Counseling with mothers of exceptional children. *Elementary School Guidance and Counseling*, 6:1, 32-36, Oct. 1971.

It is possible for elementary school guidance counselors to help mothers of exceptional children face the severe reality demands they experience, and shown as internal turmoil, anger, guilt, and self-depreciation. The counselor who is sensitive to the reality basis for the mother's feelings can provide help. Once the relationship is established, the mother can be made to understand the reasons for her feelings. Periodic help is needed as the children grow and develop.

Kass, Corrine: Advanced institute for leadership personnel in learning disabilities: Tucson, Arizona, 1969. *J of Learn Disabil*, 4:8, 453-455, Oct. 1971.

The participants of the institute met to discuss the upgrading of leadership personnel in L.D. through the exchange of information and through contact with ideas about teaching and learning from disciplines other than special education.

The discussions were concerned with first, specific roles and functions of the teachers in L.D. and second, implications for preparing such personnel.

Keirn, William C.: Shopping parents: Patient problem or professional problem? *Ment Retard*, 9:4, 6-7, Aug. 1971.

The term "shopping parent" has been applied in various ways that are confusing. The author decided to define the term and test the hypothesis about the parents "shopping." On a basis of 218 families surveyed, less than 3 percent were seen as shopping parents and these parents were making a specific request of the clinic. The author offers several suggestions as to how parents can be assisted and concluded that the term "shopping parent" is a misnomer.

In conclusion, it would appear that the term "shopping parent" is really a misnomer in that the parent does not simply flit from one professional to another, rejecting recommendations and information. Rather, it has been suggested that such misnamed parents come to professionals requesting different services than those they have had previously. They can best be helped by meeting that request.

Kenney, Eleanore T.: A diagnostic pre-school for atypical children. *Except Child*, 36:3, 193-199, Nov. 1969.

The Miriam School, St. Louis, provides a diagnostic preschool with the goal of helping each child to realize maximal intellectual potential. The program consists of three phases or goals. Primary is the diagnosis of developmental patterns of the child in assessing emotional, visual motor, auditory and vocal levels of development. The next phase is the active intervention and tailoring of a developmental program to enhance strengths and compensate for weaknesses. The final phase is to work jointly with parents to help the children function in the home and the community.

A battery of tests helps formulate the curriculum for each child. The child is then placed in a class of approximately six children with a teacher and a volunteer aide. The grouping is behaviorally heterogeneous. Family counseling consists of monthly meetings with the mothers.

Progress is measured by readministration of tests. Longitudinal studies illustrate that the most important goals realized by the children and the preschool are in the areas of school achievement and emotional adjustment.

Kolstoe, Oliver M.: Programs for the mildly retarded: A reply to the critics. *Except Child*, 39:1, 51-55, Sept. 1972.

Park, Jeanne S.: They're sharing something special. *American Education*, 5:3, 23-25, March 1969.

The county school system of Richmond, Georgia, has optimized usage of Title I of the ESEA to benefit handicapped learners. Administrators use funds from the general Title I guidelines to complement funds allocated for handicapped learners also served by Title I funds. The result is that over $700 is spent on each handicapped learner; this is nearly $170 more than the amount spent on "normal" learners. In addition, the system has adopted innovative approaches to the instruction of handicapped learners. This mixture of ideas and dollars makes for a productive system.

Payne, R., and Murray, C.: Principals' attitudes toward integration of the handicapped. *Except Child*, 41:2, 123-125, Oct. 1974.

The school building principal, because of his leadership role, should be considered a key person in initiating the integration of the handicapped into regular classrooms. The authors report that urban elementary principals are more reluctant to integrate handicapped children than are their suburban counterparts. There appears to be more administrative support for such activity in the suburban schools.

Reger, Roger, and Koppman, Marian: The child oriented resource room. *Except Child*, 37:6, 460-462, Feb. 1971.

The article describes an experimental resource room implemented in Buffalo, New York. It was a program operated by the Board of Cooperative Educational Services (BOCES). A total of eleven resource rooms for learning disabilities and educable mentally handicapped students was established in the 1969-70 school year, and in the 1970-71 school year the program grew to twenty-three resource rooms. The resource rooms are located in regular elementary and secondary buildings. A space about the size of a small classroom is used. No child can be in the resource room more than a half day at a time. If it is determined that more time is needed, the child is then placed in a special class. A major advantage of the resource room approach is that the children are assigned to regular classes and thus easily assimilated into the school's mainstream.

Roche, Adam, Jr., and Neal, W. R., Jr.: State certification policies and procedures for the hearing impaired. *Volta Review,* 74:3, 150-160, March 1972.

The authors reported on a study made to determine the extent to which State Departments of Education are recognizing, through certification, areas of specialty in serving the hearing impaired.

Only eighteen states offered certification in audiology, with seventeen of them having an audiologist in their employ. There are a total of 489 audiologists employed across the nation. Five states indicated that licensing was required by the state for public school work as an audiologist.

Public schools are continuing to improve the quality and quantity of service to the hearing impaired. These services lag behind services offered to children having only speech disorders. It is felt that more professionals would be employed if states would adopt certification that would allow reimbursement.

Sabatino, David A.: An evaluation of resource rooms for children with learning disabilities. *J Learn Disabil,* 4:2, 84-93, Feb. 1971.

The author describes the use of resource rooms as instructional centers for children with learning disabilities and compares them to self-contained special classes. He points out that many children achieved as well in a resource room as in a special class.

The resource room is another way to group children with learning disabilities which causes less labeling than placement in a special class.

Scholl, Geraldine T.: *The Principal Works with the Visually Impaired.* Council for Exceptional Children Monograph, Washington, D.C., 1968, 1-62.

Scholl gives a brief overview of programs for the visually impaired and provides some practical suggestions for principals who may have such programs in their buildings. The monograph contains a listing of the most commonly used resources when help is needed for the visually impaired which is not readily available at the local level or which can supplement local resources.

Schultz, Edward W., Hurschoren, Alfred, Manton, Ann B., and Henderson, Robert A.: Special education for the emotionally disturbed. *Except Child*, 38:4, 313-321, Dec. 1971.

A questionnaire on the status of public school services for emotionally disturbed children was sent out to the fifty states to inquire about the eligibility, definitions, and basic program standards for programs. There seemed to be a lack of concensus in terminology and definition, but it is clearly seen that there is an evaluation of services which are needed. One optimistic finding was that the trend is away from having a single diagnostician determine eligibility to using a team composed of both mental health specialists and education specialists, along with parent involvement.

The percentage of children reported being returned to the regular classroom ranged from 5 to 90 percent. It was stressed that there is a need to bring order to the efforts of the educators, especially on evaluation. Careful and systematic record keeping is advised.

Schultz, Edward, Manton, Anne, and Salvia, John: Screening emotionally disturbed children in a rural setting. *Except Child*, 39:3, 134-137, Oct. 1972.

The authors described a study undertaken to determine the effectiveness of screening procedures for emotionally disturbed children. The study involved two county rural areas in eastern central Illinois. The question of interpersonal bias in screening procedures was studied, as well as the correlation between a set of materials for screening problems and the ratings of problem children and the ratings of problem behaviors. The study found that teacher or student screening was not biased by the absence of interpersonal compatibility. It was also found that there was a significant relationship between childhen identified as potentially disturbed and ratings of problem behaviors.

Schultz, Jerome J.: Integration of emotionally disturbed students: The role of the director of special education. *Except Child*, 40:1, 39-41, Sept. 1973.

More positive communication is needed between the director of special education and the regular school staff. To help make this possible a list of twelve suggestions for a director to follow is presented.

The author attempts to close the gap in knowledge felt by the regular school staff regarding emotionally disturbed children.

Schwartz, Louis: A clinical teacher model for interrelated areas of special education. *Except Child,* 37:8, 565-571, April 1971.

The author describes a teacher preparation program designed for interrelated areas in special education rather than the usual categorical approach to teacher training.

Shores, Richard, and Haubrich, Paul: Effects of cubicles in educating emotionally disturbed children. *Except Child,* 36:1, 21-24, Sept. 1969.

Cubicles are considered an aid in reducing the amount of irrelevant stimuli to which some atypical children are believed to overreact. However, research has not demonstrated that cubicles do accelerate learning.

The authors indicate that cubicles influence attending behavior, but do not show immediate effects on academic achievement. However, principals and administrators tend to believe that teachers are better instructors because they use cubicles and thus cut down on the occurrences of deviant behavior.

Smith, William L.: Ending isolation of the handicapped. *American Education,* 7:9, 29-33, Nov. 1971.

The author discusses the necessity of teaching teachers how to spot the child with learning disabilities early in the child's career and how to recognize the home environment factors which trigger or accelerate the disability. The article goes on to discuss training the teacher in special teaching skills and materials that have proved most effective in helping the child with a handicap to overcome the handicap or get an education despite the handicap. The author then describes a program funded by the Office of Education under the Education Professions Development Act (EPDA) which offers in-service training programs for teachers and other school staff. The training programs for EPDA are based on research that indicates that many handicapped children learn just as fast or faster in normal situations as they do in isolated self-contained classrooms, and that most self-contained classrooms for the handicapped do not justify the cost involved. The EPDA funded training in special education stresses that for every weakness a child is apt to have a compensating strength, and teachers are trained to build on that strength so that the child will likely succeed despite his handicap. The article concludes by describing two underlying elements in the EPDA design strategy: 1) a humanistic approach to education and 2) an individual approach to learning.

Sparks, Howard L., and Davis, Sue M.: Administrative practices in junior and senior high school programs for educable mentally retarded. *Ed and Tr of the Ment Retard, 4*:3, 119-121, Oct. 1969.

The authors conducted a survey to gain information on current status of secondary public school programs as they relate to instruction of educable mentally retarded students. There was no attempt to do a qualitative analysis of the programs, rather they tried to determine existent administrative practices and policies. The survey clearly showed that the majority of students are attending regular school with their chronological peer group. Only 70 percent of the EMR students at the secondary level are in self-contained classrooms. Many of the students were receiving certificates rather than diplomas when they completed their training.

Stephens, Thomas and Birch, Jack: Merits of special class, resource, and itinerant plans for teaching partially seeing children. *Except Child, 35*:6, 481-485, Feb. 1969.

This article provides a review of the literature concerning the advantages and disadvantages of three organizational schemes for teaching partially sighted students. These three forms were: 1) full time special class—all instruction is with a special teacher, 2) resource teacher—student is assigned to a regular class but goes to a resource room for special instruction and 3) itinerant teacher—a teacher who travels from school to school giving special instruction.

Basically, the literature is inconclusive; no significant difference exists between the effectiveness of the three forms.

Streng, Alice: Public school programs for children with impaired hearing in small school systems. *Except Child, 25*:2, 71-76, Oct. 1958.

The author indicates that the prevalence of children with impaired hearing varies with estimates varying from 5 to 30 per 1000.

Good school programs for hard of hearing children are dependent upon: 1) supportive and permissive administrative policy, 2) effective and efficient case-finding procedures, 3) thorough diagnostic and evaluative audiological services, and 4) a sufficient number of well-trained teachers. The key to success is cooperation between the many agencies and persons who have an impact on the hard of hearing.

Striefel, Sabastian: Television as a language training medium with retarded children. *Ment Retard, 10:2,* 27-29, April 1972.

This article is a review of the research being done which used television for training the retarded. The data suggest that television is a potentially useful training medium, but one which is yet to be completely explored. Specific suggestions for research in the use of television for training prelanguage and language skills are included, along with a suggestion that training tapes for national viewing be developed.

Talkington, Larry W.: Outreach: Delivery of services to rural communities. *Ment Retard, 9:5,* 27-29, Oct. 1971.

This article introduces the reader to a new approach for delivering services to the retarded in rural communities. The institutional staff and facilities are used as backup resources. The outreach team works through community personnel to stimulate program development with a focus on growth of community-centered resources.

Tannenbaum, Abraham J.: *Special Education and Programs for Disadvantaged Children and Youth.* Council for Exceptional Children Monograph, Washington, D.C., 1968, 1-129.

The chapters are made up from a series of papers which were presented at a conference conducted in Washington in 1967 by the Council for Exceptional Children. Various experts in the education of exceptional children related the problems of a specific area to the whole problem of social disadvantage.

Tenorio, Sue, and Raimist, Lewis: A noncategorical consortium program. *Except Child, 38:4,* 325-326, Dec. 1971.

A well-written and informative article dealing with the consolidation of special education programs in three northern Virginia communities. Under a $79,000 Title III grant a consortium was formed. In addition, two new teacher models were implemented. These being: 1) diagnostic prescriptive model, and 2) crisis resource model. These moves were based on three assumptions: 1) Labeling is unnecessary, 2) classes should not be segregated, and 3) the psychomedical model was not relevant. The project results lead to the conclusion that "problem students can be maintained with modifications of methods and materials in regular classes via consultative and supportive services."

Tillman, Rodney: Is ability grouping taking schools the wrong direction? *Nation's Schools,* 73:4, 70-128, April 1964.

The author argues yes. He feels grouping by ability is not a way to increase achievement, that teachers tend to teach their classes as a group rather than individually, that grouping is often influenced by socioeconomic status, that kids get labels, that pressures by parents are placed upon the "high" groups, that strain upon staff relationship often results, and that there are reduced opportunities to learn from each other.

Each of these concerns has real application for administrators and teachers in special education.

Todd, Thomas W.: Supplying meaningful educational data to diagnostic clinics. *Ment Retard,* 9:4, 10-11, Aug. 1971.

The retrieval of useful educational data is imperative if diagnostic evaluations and recommendations are to be realistic and meaningful. This article delineates some of the difficulties in retrieving educational data and suggests specific educational information that is useful to diagnostic clinics.

Valett, Robert: The learning resource center for exceptional children. *Except Child,* 36:7, 527-530, March 1970.

The Sacramento Public Schools, under Title VI of ESEA, developed a program of consulting services to teachers. The objective of the program was to stimulate the development of prescriptive teaching approaches by providing supplemental services to the usual special education programs. Priority was given to the multiply handicapped with significant learning disabilities and for whom the existing educational programs were inadequate.

A team of specialists was located in a regular elementary school. A psychoeducational specialist was director of the program. The other four members of the team included: consulting psychologist (for assisting staff, parents, and teachers), educational therapist (direct therapy for the children on an appointment basis), educational psychologist (assists in educational planning, special evaluation and parent groups), and a demonstration teacher (aids teachers in developing exemplary programs and works with selected students). It should be noted that all five members of the team worked directly with children, and that additional classes were not necessary.

The prime goal, believed to have been realized by this program, was to provide teachers, psychologists, and coordinators with consulting services. Services included the individualization of programs with special materials, flexible scheduling, behavior modification, parent involvement and counseling, and planning classroom strategies.

Vergason, Glenn A.: Accountability in special education. *Except Child,* 39:5, 367-373, Feb. 1973.

The literature on accountability was reviewed in both general and special education. It is implied that special education has been more accountable than other areas of education, but needs to do much better.

Areas suggested that could result in increased accountability are: 1) performance contracts, 2) legal cases, 3) mandatory programs, 4) voucher systems, 5) special interest organizations, 6) personal accountability, 7) better prepared teachers, and 8) administrative accountability.

At the date of writing, thirteen state legislatures were considering legislation concerning accountability.

Watson, Richard: The principal's responsibility in relation to court decisions involving public education. *High School Journal,* 53:5, 323-332, Feb. 1970.

The author indicates that courts are not eager to interfere with the management and operation of the schools and will render decisions only upon invitation. Ordinarily, courts will not intervene in the peaceful exercise of those powers unless there has been an invasion of someone's constitutional rights or the Board has acted in an unfitting manner. Courts are concerned with the legality of a decision, not administrative soundness. Actions of individual school principals and not Board policies, as such, cause court action. The author suggests that it is the responsibility of principals to utilize court decisions as guides for everyday activities as they work to carry out their legal charge.

Weinstein, Laura: Project re-ed for emotionally disturbed children: Effectiveness as viewed by referring agents, parents, and teachers. *Except Child*, 35:7, 703-711, May 1969.

The author reported that the referring agents, parents, and teachers felt the project was a success for the majority of the students involved because they displayed fewer symptoms, were more socially competent, and were more relaxed and less aggressive. However, the author stated that more research was needed to see if any improvements were due to a halo effect, increased age, or variations of behavior which occur with the passage of time.

Wille, Louis: Room for miracles. *American Education*, 6:7, 7-10, Aug. 1969.

An article relating a radical approach to educating learners with behavior disorders. The Ray School, near Chicago University, has a wide mixture of students from various ethnic groups and nationalities as well as abilities. The author discusses the formation of the Independent Learning Center and how both administrative personnel and parents combined resources to acquire funds for the program. The lesson to be learned from this article is how a community educated to the realities of exceptional learners can serve as a power base for program implementation.

Willenberg, Ernest P.: Critical issues in special education: Internal organization. *Except Child*, 33:7, 511, 512, March 1967.

The author reports that a survey (Hodgson, 1964) failed to find major trends or agreement about the best form or type of internal organization to serve exceptional children. He then suggests that centralized units are needed to provide for the planning, development and coordination of special education. Internal organization should: 1) support the ebb and flow of student placement, 2) supply instructional resources and other services as needed.

The unit of service is the individual child and his changing requirements. The goal is the optimum education and rehabilitation of each child; therefore, the system should facilitate flexible programming and should attract a child toward progressive levels of independence and self-direction. The author then suggests a scheme of internal organization for school districts.

Yates, James R.: Models for preparing regular classroom teachers for "Mainstreaming." *Except Child, 39*:6, 471-472, March 1973.

A report of a study dealing with the results of a laboratory-experimental approach to training regular teachers for dealing with special education students mainstreamed into their classrooms. The results indicated that a laboratory type preparatory course would be most beneficial for regular class teachers who would be having handicapped children "mainstreamed" in their classes. This approach was superior to the traditional "lecture" one finds in most in-service education.

GENERAL ADMINISTRATION

Bernays, Edward L.: Enlisting public support for special education programs. *J Ed, 152*:1, 56-58, Oct., 1969.

There is a wide gap between the expert's knowledge of how to deal with the handicapped child and the public's awareness of the problem and its willingness to cope with it. It is the gap between these two poles that he wants to bridge.

Bernays believes that the special education instructional centers in the United States have helped increase public acceptance of special education programs.

He also believes that through taking a series of steps, educators can "engineer" consent from the public for increases in special education funds. Such steps must include definition of short- and long-range objectives, determination of strategy, design of appeals which will elicit public support, establishment of an organization to carry out activities, and finally, the planning of action to meet the goals of the program. This last step involves working with three key elements of society in order to close the gap between expert knowledge and public action. The elements to be included are educational groups, social, political, and professional leaders, and opinion molders. The opinion molders include all the media.

It is, the author believes, debatable whether or not the instructional materials centers have had any effect on the public. It is doubtful that most of the public even knows about them. Bernay's remarks concerning the use of power blocs are the most relevant and useful of all his suggestions.

Blatt, Burton: Public policy and the education of children with special needs. *Except Child,* 38:7, 537-545, March 1972.

Public policy needs a great deal of revamping to provide adequately for the needs of children.

Labelling should emphasize the child's development needs rather than his deviancy.

Funding has too often "passed the buck" to private services rather than community based services.

Parental involvement must be secured to help in securing appropriate services for their children.

Bruno, Marvin, and O'Brien, Gary: A survey of public relations practices in public and private residential facilities for the mentally retarded. *Mental Retardation,* 8:6, 36-40, Dec. 1970.

Questionnaires were sent to a random sample of institutions (both public and private) listed in the 1968 *Directory of Residential Facilities for the Mentally Retarded.*

Part I of the questionnaire was concerned with group tours and their relative importance as a public relations project.

Part II was concerned with open house and parent visitation.

Part III was concerned with other public relations activities.

Part IV asked the respondents to rate nine public relations projects and eight types of articles in newsletters according to importance as public relations activities.

The total return of the questionnaires was 76.5 percent

resulting in a good overview of the public relations practices in institutions for the mentally retarded across the country.

Bullock, Lyndal M.: An inquiry into the special education training of elementary school administrators. *Except Child*, 36:10, 770-771, Summer 1970.

Special educators often express concern about the lack of administrative support. A review of certification requirements for the United States (fifty states, D.C. and Puerto Rico) showed that none require elementary school administrators to take special education courses.

Unless the administrator elected to take a course in exceptional children he would have little formal background to guide his decision making.

To test this hypothesis and to determine the amount of special education training that elementary administrators had, a survey of ninety-two in a large midwestern school district revealed: 65 percent with no special education course work related to exceptional child, 23 percent with one course, 8 percent with two courses, and 4 percent three or more courses. Unless it is required it appears that few elementary administrators will take courses in special education.

Elementary administrators' attitudes toward the exceptional child are very important for the success of special education programs. Wholesome attitudes can be facilitated by dissemination of information which in turn can lead to understanding, acceptance, and action.

The author proposes that universities include special education training for all administrators in training, and that states require such training in their certification codes.

Burrello, Leonard, and Sage, Daniel: A behavior preference inventory for special education administrators. *Except Child*, 37:1, 365-369, January 1971.

This article deals with a study undertaken by the authors in hopes of developing an instrument capable of measuring the need value of groups of administrators. The Behavior Preference Inventory was proven valid and appears to have potential for sensitizing all administrators to personality investments involved in decision-making processes, for it is believed that personality factors have a major influence on administrative decisions. In addition, the authors feel that certain factors need be uncovered, which may dissuade certain persons from seeking administrative roles.

Connor, Leo E.: Preparation programs for special education administrators. *Except Child,* 33:3, 161-167, Nov. 1966.

Connor reflects considerable doubt as to whether graduate research and theory activities and upgraded requirements in universities are effectively creating a true profession of special education administrators. Literature reviews by Kirk, Gallagher, and others, demonstrate little interest in specifying and up-grading standards of preparation. Connor outlines what he considers to be a more meaningful preparatory program with the major emphasis directed toward in-depth study in the field of education, together with a cross-section of the behavioral and social sciences. His minimum program consists of a B.A. in education, a 40-50 hr. M.A. in special education, two or three years teaching experience with exceptional children, and thirty postmasters hours.

Henley, Charles E.: A view of the field experience in special education administration. *Except Child,* 37:4, 275-281, Dec. 1970.

The field placement is one of the universal elements presently found in USOE supported college and university programs for the preparation of special education administrators. There are several types and have been given descriptive titles such as: "Field Experience" in which students visit and observe, but perform no actual duties; "Internship" which comes at or near the completion of the student's formal program of preparation. This type involves a considerable block of time and involves a continuous administrative position in the field under competent supervision of a practicing administrator. The author describes a program at Michigan State University in which the students participate in one internship and two practicum placements. A number of observations resulted from four years' experience with this program. 1) The interaction of people in unique settings cannot be accurately programmed or predicted in advance. 2) The college professor is limited in his ability to be a supervisor of the field placement. 3) The success of the field placement depends primarily upon two factors, the strength of the supervising administrator and the strength of the student. 4) Administrators at all levels are interested in the field placement program and are willing to give time and effort to assist its operation.

Kipfer, Bernice: Conceptualizing an administration/management system for special education. *Educational Technology,* 8:6, 16-21, June 1973.

A review of the Special Education Department of Syracuse, New York is presented in this article. The background of the system is discussed, then the entire model is described, both in written form and with flow charts. The model includes a brief description of each area of handicap and the types of services available. Processes for initial referral, determining transportation, arranging placement, and evaluating the outcomes are also included.

McKenzie, Hugh; Egnor, Ann; Knight, Mareta; Perelman, Phyllis; Schneider, Betsy, and Garvin, Jean: Training consulting teachers to assist elementary teachers in the management and education of handicapped children. *Except Child,* 37:2, 137-143, Oct. 1970.

The authors describe a graduate program designed to train consulting teachers. Major emphasis is placed on the application and utilization of behavior modification. Three case studies are cited to further clarify the benefits of such a training program.

McNamara, Blanche H.: Organization of a staff library. *Ment Retard,* 10:4, 8-10, Aug. 1972.

The results of a questionnaire sent to 150 institutions for the mentally retarded in the United States reveal that 102 have staff libraries of varying qualities, with only thirty having a professional librarian in charge. Better staff libraries may result if administrators understood the basic requirements for, and advantages in library service. This paper explains how a library was organized, and offers suggestions derived from experience on how to provide its many services by discussing the following areas: 1) Securing a professional librarian, 2) selecting a library committee, 3) financing, 4) choosing a classification system, and 5) rendering services to the staff and the community.

Marge, Michael: Planning and evaluation for the future. *Except Child,* 34:7, 505-508, March 1968.

This article demonstrates the need for program planning and evaluation for education, more specifically, special education. An office was set up under the Bureau of Education for the Handicapped to plan the program and spell out the evaluation functions. Functions for the office are presented and discussed.

Marro, T. D., and Kohl, J. W.: Normative study of the administrative position in special education. *Except Child,* 39:1, 5-13, Sept. 1972.

The expansion of special education programs has created the need for more special education administrators. However, there is currently an insufficient training base for the people filling these positions.

This study investigates the particular characteristics of special education administration in order to provide guidelines for the training of special education administrators.

The following elements of administration were investigated: 1) characteristics of the administrator of special education, 2) experience, preparation, certification and association membership, 3) conditions of employment, 4) role in program administration and supervision, 5) organizational characteristics and programming elements, and 6) selected administrative opinions.

Meyen, Edward L.: A statewide system approach to inservice training for teachers of the mentally retarded. *Except Child,* 35:5, 353-357, Jan. 1969.

Inservice training for teachers of the mentally retarded was felt to be necessary due to the lack of well-defined instructional objectives, lack of sequential porgrams and omission of in-service training within the various school systems.

It was determined that to be effective, the following factors must be included in the statewide system: 1) decision making relating to content must be sensitive to the needs expressed by the teachers, 2) the training must routinely involve all teachers on a frequent basis, and 3) the training must lead to the development of consultative services.

The system adopted by the state utilized the master teacher concept as an in-service educator. Master teachers (those with teaching experience and a Master's degree) were selected by the various geographic areas within the state. In conjunction with a university, the Special Education Curriculum Center was established to train and aid these master teachers.

Newman, Karen S.: Administrative tasks in special education. *Except Child, 36*:7, 521-524, March 1966.

Newman conducted a survey of the functional tasks of special education administration in 100 randomly selected school districts with pupil populations between 13,000 and 30,000. The major findings were: 1) Programming for the gifted is not included in special education services in most school districts (most emphasis is on the mentally retarded). 2) Research on improvement and clarification of programs is not being done. 3) There appears to be a direct relationship between training in the education of exceptional children and performance of the administrative tasks of planning and directing in-service meetings and workshops. 4) There appears to be a direct relationship between experience in special education teaching and performance of the administrative tasks of curriculum planning and teacher evaluation. 5) The survey seemed to validly select the common tasks of special education administration.

Reger, Roger: How can we influence teacher-training programs. *J Spec Ed, 8*:1, 7-13, Spring 1974.

The point is made that there has been little input from public school administrators in the training process. He suggests the use of advisory boards to provide a systematic input from the field to teacher training institutions.

Sage, Daniel: Functional emphasis in special education administration. *Except Child, 35*:1, 69-70, Sep. 1968.

A comparison was made between administrators of regular programs and those in special education. Special education administrators indicated that they spent 40 percent of their time on program development, 27 percent on personnel development, and 16 percent on community activities. By comparison with regular administrators they spent significantly more time on technical skills and less on human skills.

Shafter, Albert J.: A philosophy of administration: A revisit. *Ment Retard*, 9:5, 3-5, Oct. 1971.

The author describes how administrators of residential facilities have been under attack for dehumanizing "lower-level" employees. As a result there is a caste system existing among the staff. He specifies that it is a fact that administrators and professionals tend to dehumanize the so-called nonprofessional employees. Until the dehumanization process with direct care personnel is stopped the job of ending dehumanization of the residents shall not be completed.

Valletutti, Peter J.: Administrative responsibility in implementing special education programs. *Maryland Teacher*, 26-27, May 1969.

Given the realization of the importance of special education, the administrator must strive to implement an effective special education program. He can secure adequate services by taking an active role in: teacher education, curriculum planning, obtaining funds, textbook approval and innovations in methodology.

Overall, the administrator must be aware of the needs and strive to incorporate them into the school's special education program.

Vergason, G., Smith, F., and Wyatt, K.: Questions for administrators about special education. *Theory into Practice. 14*:2, 99-104, April 1975.

The authors provide a brief overview regarding the complexity of the special education administrative scene. They then proceed to ask questions and provide dialogue for some of the pressing concerns as they see them. Their questions are loaded with what, why, and who, but the technique discusses a forum for getting to hot topics while also providing for and seeking a common philosophical base. This article provides a refreshing look at current problems.

Willenberg, Ernest P.: Administration of special education: Aspects of a professional problem. *Except Child, 30*:5, 194-195, Jan. 1964.

At the time this paper was written, it appeared that there was a growing concern that colleges and universities were not preparing leadership personnel with the basic tools of instruction (a textbook on the subject had yet to be published). Research in the area was encouraged because no single source of comprehensive information providing a rationale, structure and process for the administration of special education programs had been developed.

The author proposed ten areas of research that would be oriented around problems that exist in the field. They were: 1) nature and scope of programs and services, 2) structure, organization, and relationship of instructional services for exceptional children, 3) instrumentalities for program planning, development, and coordination, 4) provisions for recruitment, deployment, and in-service training of personnel, 5) supervision of instruction including horizontal and vertical articulation of pupil personnel, 6) financing of special education, preparation of budgets, and the control of expenditures, 7) planning of facilities and use of supplies and equipment, 8) provision of transportation, food, and other ancillary services, 9) evaluation and interpretation of the special program for purposes of pupil guidance and public information, 10) areas of administrative research activity and application of research findings.

Willower, Donald J.: Special education: Organization and administration. *Except Child*, 36:8, 591-594, April 1970.

The author compares special education administration to "a virgin untouched by the concerns" of theory and bureaucracy or other organizational behavior. School policies call for periodic review of special education, but no formal administrative mechanism exists to carry out such reviews. The author calls for inquiry into viewing special education as a subculture of the general school and also calls for evaluating special education teachers' social position within the larger teacher group. He points out two barriers to making the necessary inquiry. They are: 1) analysis may appear to be threatening to those people involved, 2) traditional measurement and experiments will find inquiries into some latent functions to be imprecise.

Wisland, Milton V., and Vaughan, Tony D.: Administrative problems in special education. *Except Child*, 31:1, 87-89, Oct. 1964.

This study had a two-fold purpose of 1) identifying and describing the kinds of problems experienced by directors and supervisors of special education programs in thirteen western

APPENDIX

THE COUNCIL FOR EXCEPTIONAL CHILDREN • 1920 Association Drive • Reston, Va. 22091
STATE STATUTORY RESPONSIBILITIES FOR THE EDUCATION OF HANDICAPPED CHILDREN

July 1, 1975

This chart was prepared by The Development and Evaluation of State and Local Special Education Administrative Policy Manuals

162

states, a
between
length o

A co
rating b
problem

The
between
conclud
adminis
or exper

State	Type of Mandation	Date of Passage	Compliance Date	Ages of Eligibility	Categories Excluded
Louisiana	Court Order—Orleans Parish only: Selective for Mentally Retarded. Otherwise, Mandatory	1972	1972	3-21[10]	Other than Mentally Retarded
Maine	Full Planning and Programming	1973	1975[11]	5-20	
Maryland	Full Planning and Programming	1973	1979[12]	[13]	
Massachusetts	Full Planning and Programming	1972		3-21	
Michigan	Full Planning and Programming	1971	9/73	Birth-25	
Minnesota	Full Program	7/72[14]	[14]	4-21, except MR (5-21) and ED (6-21)	
Mississippi	Permissive	1973		Birth-21	
Missouri	Full Planning and Programming	1973		5-21	
Montana	Full Program[15]	1974		6-21	
Nebraska	Full Planning and Programming	1973	7/79	5-18	
Nevada	Full Program	1973	10/76[16]	5-18[17]	
New Hampshire	Full Program			Birth-21	
New Jersey	Full Program	1954[18]		5-20	
New Mexico	Full Planning and Programming	1972	9/76	6-21[19]	
New York	Full Program	1973	1973	5-21	
North Carolina	Full Planning	1974	[20]	Birth-Adulthood[21]	
North Dakota	Full Planning and Programming	1973	7/80[22]	5-21[3]	
Ohio	Permissive			Birth-21	
	Selective Planning	1972	1973	[23]	Other than crippled or Educable Mentally Retarded, Deaf, Blind, Partial hearing or vision; Trainable or Profoundly Mentally Retarded
Oklahoma	Full Program	1971	9/70	4-21[24]	Profoundly Retarded
Oregon	Full Program	1973		EMR: 6-21 Others: Birth-21	
Pennsylvania	Court Order: Selective (Mentally Retarded Only)	1972	9/72	6-21[25]	Other than mentally retarded
	Full Planning and Programming	1956	1956	6-21	

Rhode Island...Full Program...........	1972	1964[26]	3-21[26]
South Carolina...Full Planning and Programming...........	1972	1977	6-21[27]
South Dakota...Full Program...........	1972		Birth-21
Tennessee.........Full Planning and Programming...........	1972	9/74[2]	4-21
Utah..............Full Program[28]...........	1969	9/76[28]	3-21
Vermont...........Full Program[29]...........	1972		5-21
Virginia..........Full Planning...........	1972		Birth-21
Washington.......Full Program...........	1971	[30]	2-21
West Virginia...Full Program...........	1974		6-21[31]
Wisconsin.........Full Planning and Programming...........	1973	1974	5-23[32]
Wyoming.........Full Program...........	1969	8/74	3-21

[1]Current statute is conditional: 5 or more similarly handicapped children in district. However, a 1973 Attorney General's opinion stated that the law mandating full planning and programming was effective July, 1973. If the state activates a kindergarten program for 5-year-old children, ages of eligibility will be 5-21.

[2]Permissive for children 3-21, except MR: 5 yrs. 8 mos.-21.

[3]3-21 for hearing impaired. Lower figure applies to age of child as of Jan. 1 of the school year.

[4]1973 law did not include profoundly retarded; however, a 1974 amendment brought these children under the provisions of the mandatory law. Compliance date for full services to these children is mandated for 1977-78.

[5]Earlier (1963) law was mandatory for all handicapped children except Trainable Mentally Retarded.

[6]5-21 for speech defective.

[7]Permissive 3-5 and 19-21.

[8]"Developmentally Disabled" means retardation, cerebral palsy or epilepsy. For other disabilities, the state board is to determine ages of eligibility as part of the state plan. Compliance date is 7/1/74 for DD programs.

[9]Permissive: 3-6.

[10]Residents over age 21 who were not provided educational services as children must also be given education and training opportunities.

[11]In cases of significant hardship the commissioner of education may waive enforcement until 1977.

[12]Court order sets deadline in Sept., 1975.

[13]Services must begin as soon as the child can benefit from them, whether or not he is of school age.

[14]Date on which Trainable Mentally Retarded were included under the previously existing mandatory law.

[15]Statute now in effect is selective and conditional: at least 10 Educable Mentally Retarded, 7 Trainable Mentally Retarded, or 10 physically handicapped in school district. *Full* mandate becomes effective 7/1/79.

[16]Acoustically handicapped: birth-18.

[17]Aurally handicapped and visually handicapped: birth-18.

[18]Date of original mandatory law, which has since been amended to include all children.

[19]Child must be 6 years old by Jan. 1 of school year.

[20]Implementation date to be specified in preliminary state plan to be submitted to 1975 General Assembly.

[21]Deaf: to age 18—or to age 21 "if need exists."

[22]All children must be served as soon as they are identified as handicapped.

[23]Deaf children to be served at age four.

[24]2-21 for blind, partially blind, deaf, hard of hearing.

[25]When programs are provided for pre-school age children they must also be provided for mentally handicapped children of the same age.

[26]For mentally retarded or multiply handicapped. Others, as defined in regulations. Compliance date established by regulations.

[27]4-21 for hearing handicapped. The Texas Educational Agency is operating under the assumption that the law is mandatory, and has requested an opinion from the state Attorney General on this question. Compliance date is as established by state policy if the law does not specify a compliance date.

[28]Within the limits of available funds and personnel.

[29]9/1/76 established by regulations.

[30]Permissive below 6 years.

[31]Permissive 3-4.

Definition of the kinds of mandatory legislation used by states:

Full Program Mandate: Such laws require that programs must be provided where children meet the criteria defining the exceptionality.

Planning and Programming Mandate: This form includes required planning prior to required programming.

Planning Mandate: This kind of law mandates only a requirement for planning.

Conditional Mandate: This kind of law requires that certain conditions must be met in or by the local education district before mandation takes effect (this usually means that a certain number of children with like handicaps must reside in a district before the district is obliged to provide for them).

Mandate by Petition: This kind of law places the burden of responsibility for program development on the community in terms of parents and interested agencies who may petition school districts to provide programs.

Selective Mandate: In this case, not all disabilities are treated equally. Education is provided (mandated) for some, but not all categories of disabilities.

The work performed herein was done pursuant to a grant from the Bureau of Education for the Handicapped, U.S. Office of Education, Department of Health, Education, and Welfare. The opinions expressed herein, however, do not necessarily reflect the position or policy of the U.S. Office of Education, and no official endorsement by the U.S. Office of Education should be inferred.

NAME INDEX

167

SUBJECT INDEX

A

Accountability, 137, 151
Administration, 153-162 (bibliography)
  cooperative arrangements, 27, 29
    (Illinois)
  directors and supervisors, 43-45
  federal, 25-27
  intermediate school district, 27-28
    (Michigan)
  local, 30-31
  special education service areas
    (SESA), 29
  special school district, 29-30
    (St. Louis County, Mo.)
  state, 27
American Education, 50
Audiologist, 32

B

Bilingual programs, 48
Blindness, 86-90
Bureau for Education of the
    Handicapped, 26
Busing, 36-38

C

Census, handicapped, 61
Child Service Demonstration
    Programs, 119
Civic responsibility, 8, 68, 141
Council for Exceptional Children, 26,
    40
Cubicles, use of, 147
Culturally disadvantaged, 112
Curriculum
  development and improvement,
    66-68

D

Deafness, 82-85, 143
  mental retardation, and, 134-135
Diagnosis, 31-36
  education, 32
  medical, 31-32
  psychological, 32
  social, 32

E

Early childhood education, 49-50
Economic self-sufficiency, 8, 68, 141
Education Professions Development
    Act, 40, 147
Elementary and Secondary Education
    Act (P.L. 89-10), 9, 14-15, 23, 50
  Title I, 14, 117
  Title II, 14-15
  Title III, 15, 150
  Title IV, 15
  Title V, 15-16
  Title VI, 16, 117, 150
Emotional disturbances, 79-82, 145, 146
Exceptional Children journal, 6, 16, 26,
    48
Excess cost plans, 20-23
Expulsion, 17-18

F

Financing, 19-24
  federal aid, 23
  set-aside funds, 14

H

Hearing impaired, 85-86, 148
Handicapped Children's Early
    Education Act (P.L. 90-538), 143

171